U.S. Navy
SEALs
The Quiet Professionals

Carolyn & Kit Bonner

Schiffer Military/Aviation History
Atglen, PA

Dedication

The Quiet Professionals is dedicated to the men who willingly work so hard to earn the U.S. Navy Special Warfare "Trident" as SEALs, and the Special Warfare Combat Crewmembers to earn the "SWCC" insignia. They do not let up, ask for no quarter or glory, and are satisfied with the recognition of their own community of warriors. They are the best of the best, and we are proud of them beyond words. We are gratified that the U.S. Navy Special Warfare Command is there to defend our nation—now more than ever.

Acknowledgments

Special Thanks to:
- Lt. Katie Licup, USN, Assistant Public Affairs Officer, Naval Special Warfare Command
- Lt Tamsen McCabe, USN, Public Affairs Officer, Naval Special Warfare Training Center
- Andy Wilkins, SEAL Team Three
- Don Crawford, Navy Special Warfare Historian, Coronado, California
- Jim Barnes, President, Board of Directors, UDT- SEAL Museum Association, Inc, Fort Pierce, FL
- Rear Admiral Eric Olson, Commanding Officer, Naval Special Warfare Command
- George Bisharat, Naval Artist and Special Warfare Historian

For Ted

Book Design by Ian Robertson.

Printed in China.
ISBN: 0-7643-1557-9

We are interested in hearing from authors with book ideas on related topics.

Published by Schiffer Publishing Ltd.
4880 Lower Valley Road
Atglen, PA 19310
Phone: (610) 593-1777
FAX: (610) 593-2002
E-mail: Schifferbk@aol.com.
Visit our web site at: www.schifferbooks.com
Please write for a free catalog.
This book may be purchased from the publisher.
Please include $3.95 postage.
Try your bookstore first.

In Europe, Schiffer books are distributed by:
Bushwood Books
6 Marksbury Avenue
Kew Gardens
Surrey TW9 4JF
England
Phone: 44 (0) 20 8392-8585
FAX: 44 (0) 20 8392-9876
E-mail: Bushwd@aol.com.
Free postage in the UK. Europe: air mail at cost.
Try your bookstore first.

Contents

Preface

"Just What We Need, Another SEAL Book"

As we entered the parachute loft at the U.S. Naval Special Warfare Center in Coronado, California, one of the SEAL petty officers who was rigging his parachute responded to our introduction by saying, "just what we need, another SEAL book." Despite our protests that this book would be different, he remained skeptical.

Apparently, during the last few months the Special Warfare Center had been continuously inundated with network camera crews and authors who were writing or televising yet another in a seemingly endless stream of books, movies, TV specials, and magazine articles about the SEALs and their place in the American military arsenal. One particular network had set up what seemed to be permanent residence there. Most of these interviewers were seeking the heart pounding excitement of coming face to face with the enemy and killing them with stealth and violence, but due to security active SEALs are not allowed to discuss their missions until the information is declassified. Consequently, the media would

have to rely upon declassified material and an endless stream of anecdotes and tales told by retired or ex-Special Warfare personnel. The active SEALs and Combat Crew we spoke with would only describe their methods and equipment in general, and most were low key and preferred anonymity.

The U.S. Navy Special Warfare Command, which includes SEAL teams, Combat Crew, Special Warfare Units, and Special Boat Squadrons, do not operate independently. It receives its direction from the United States Special Operations Command (USSOCOM). The SEALs themselves do not just decide to mount a rescue mission, such as might have been contemplated in April 2001 when a US Navy EP-3 II Aries surveillance aircraft was forced down on a Chinese airfield. Any decision to commit American special forces must come through the national chain of command and down through the Special Operations Command to whatever operational assets are most suitable to carry out a specific assignment. This includes a response to the terrorist attacks on the World

This is a SEAL team on the beach around a rubber raft that can be inflated in just seconds and deflated in a similar time frame for concealment. The dangerous and arduous ride to the combat zone is just the beginning for a SEAL—next there is the mission and the return home safely *with the entire team*. U.S. Navy

Trade Center in New York and the Pentagon in D.C. on September 11, 2001.

The establishment of United States Special Operations Command (*USSOCOM*) was a milestone for the U.S. Military establishment, and it was not a simple task. But the Navy's Special Warfare Command, as well as their Air Force and Army counterparts, are better trained and work in greater harmony than ever before. In essence, the Special Operation Command is a combined military force within a military force.

Having watched and listened to their leaders and individual SEALs, I am proud and comforted in the knowledge that they are protecting American interests and lives. They are the best of the best, and their actions speak more loudly than any of their words. They are the quintessential *quiet professionals*.

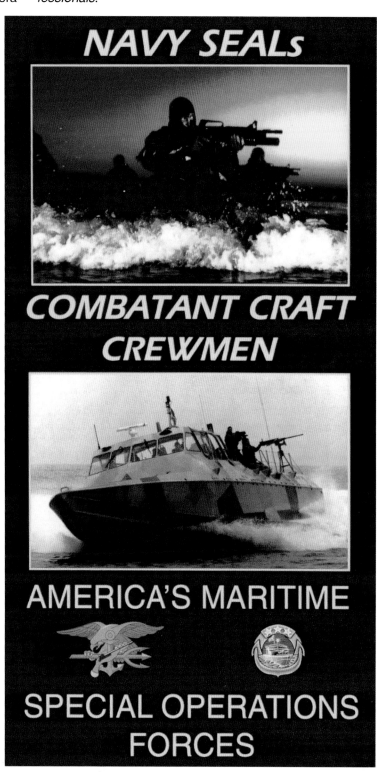

America's Maritime Special Operations Forces—Navy SEALs and Combatant (Combat) Crewmen. This is the heart and soul of U.S. Navy Special Warfare, whose combat arena is the world. In times of national emergency, these men can always be relied upon in any situation to succeed. They are renowned throughout the world as the best trained, best equipped, and best managed waterborne force. The Trident to the left is that of the SEALs, and the Combat Craft insignia is that of the *SWCC*, or Special Warfare Combat Crewmember. This pin has recently been redesigned, and those that earn it are now in a "closed loop" profession with a defined career ladder in Naval Special Warfare. SWCC has now been formally recognized service wide. These pins are the most difficult to earn in the United States or any other nation's armed forces. Only distinguishing patches worn by Air Force and U.S. Army personnel attached to USSOCOM rival them. U.S. Navy

Chapter 1

U.S. Navy Special Warfare - A Historical Perspective

Evolution of the U.S. Navy Special Warfare Command
For most Americans and generally worldwide, U.S. Navy Special Warfare comes down to one word—SEAL. This word, and the real or imagined image of these men, means the best of the best in terms of the U.S. military. If SEALs are involved in an operation, then success is almost certain to follow. However, the U.S. Navy Special Warfare Command is composed of much more than its SEAL teams. It includes one of the most rigorous training programs in the American military arsenal; a state of the art training center that evolves as need arises; a "combat think tank" in the form of a development group; patrol gunboats; special boat units; and Combat Crew. All of these components did not come together overnight. It has been an evolutionary process that began in earnest during World War II.

In August 1942 the world was embedded in war, and U.S. naval forces were becoming increasingly committed in the Pacific. Aside from defeating Germany and Italy, the Imperial Japanese Army and Navy had to be stopped from continuing advances in the Pacific. The defeat of the Japanese at Midway in June 1942 paved the way for the Allies and the American Navy to take the offensive. The choice was an island in the Solomons, and the high water mark was at Guadalcanal, where the Japanese were finally stopped in a series of bloody battles at sea and on land. It was determined that in order to retake fortified islands leading back to Japan through the Southwest and Central Pacific, a specialized force had to be created to prepare enemy beachheads prior to major amphibious landings.

The Amphibious Training Base at Little Creek, Virginia, became the site for training a reconnaissance force initially composed of Army and Navy volunteers. They became the **Reconnaissance (Amphibious) Scouts and Raiders**.

During September 1942 the first group of Scouts and Raiders, including seventeen volunteers skilled in naval salvage work, were trained in the art of demolition and overall commando operations. This one-week course barely scratched the surface of what they would need to know and ultimately face in battle, but the war could not wait. Their skills and sheer courage were needed almost immediately in "Op-

The *USS Rathburne APD-25* was at one time the four piper/flush deck destroyer *DD-113* that fought in the final months of World War I. In late April 1944 the old destroyer was modified as a fast troop transport at the Puget Sound Naval Shipyard (three inch guns mounted, two stacks removed, temporary quarters for assault or UDT personnel installed, and four sets of davits to launch shore boats). By mid September 1944 the mottled green painted ex-destroyer found herself on the way to the Palau Islands, where UDT 10 cleared the approaches to the invasion beaches. The *Rathburne* had joined an exclusive club of warships that carried frogmen to enemy beaches before the conventional, or big navy, arrived. The *Rathburne* and UDT-10 then fought their way up to the Philippines, and on one occasion the elderly vessel provided gunfire support to UDT-8, which was hurriedly leaving Anguar Island. Enough can never be said about these ships and their UDT tenants. The *USS Dallas DD-199*, which forced her way up the Wadi Sebou River with a contingent of U.S. Army Rangers in North Africa during Operation Torch, was of the same breed as the *Rathburne*. U.S.N.I.

Landing Craft Infantry (*LCI*) are beached and disembarking troops on Morotai Island. Generally, UDT teams had already been on the beach and in the waters adjacent, clearing mines and obstructions so that the assault troops and the amphibious craft had a fighting chance of establishing a beachhead. Author's Collection

A Landing Craft Tank, or *LCT*. It was on a vessel just like this that Lt (jg) Phil Bucklew steered an entire amphibious force to the correct disembarkation area at Omaha Beach on D-Day, June 6, 1944, on the Normandy coast. The tanks aboard his scout, or lead *LCT*, engaged the enemy as the ship approached the beach, and were only matched by the fire from the *LCT's* guns. Author's Collection

eration Torch," which was the Allied attack on various North African coastal areas. Just two months after being familiarized with cable cutting, obstruction removal, and demolition, they found themselves cutting a cable and other barriers across the Wadi Sebou River. This mission was necessary to allow a converted four piper destroyer, the *USS Dallas DD-199*, to carry U.S. Army Rangers up the river past the fortifications of the Kasba. The *Dallas* literally fought her way up river against one obstruction after another, including grounding, sunken block vessels, and shore battery fire. She successfully landed the Rangers, who secured the airfield at Port Lyautey, and within hours Air Corps *P-40* aircraft were using the airstrip. In essence, a combined team of specially trained naval and army personnel took a major objective as an "unofficial" Special Operations Force. The *Dallas* was awarded a Presidential Unit Citation, and at least three Navy Crosses were awarded to those who risked so much to gain the objective, including Chief Boatswains Mate Roy B Dowling, USN. Also included in this first group was Ensign *"Phil H Bucklew,"* for whom the current Naval Training Center building is named. Bucklew was an early pioneer in the Scouts and Raiders, and later won two Navy Crosses for heroism (Sicily landing) and on D-Day (Normandy). Bucklew is the acknowledged "father of Naval Special Warfare," and occupies a distinguished place in the history of this organization.

The second contingent of Scouts and Raiders was assigned tasks in the Pacific as Special Services Unit #1 on July 7, 1943, and performed well in New Guinea. The organization changed from a combined force of army and navy personnel to U.S. Navy only, and was renamed the 7th Amphibious Scouts later in 1943. This group went on to fight in forty

landings as General MacArthur's forces clawed through the southern inner rings of the defense of the Japanese Home Islands. Generally, the Amphibious Scouts would accompany the initial wave of assault craft and then destroy beach obstacles, deal with casualties, set up markers for subsequent assault craft, and perform any other tasks deemed necessary to insure a successful landing.

A third unit of Scouts and Raiders was trained at Fort Pierce, Florida, the home of the UDT-SEAL Museum. This unit included 120 officers and 900 men that were trained commando style at the newly opened Scout and Ranger School at Ft. Pierce. This unit went on to fight in China, and in concert with selected Chinese operatives surveyed the coastal areas in preparation for landings. Often this included being disguised as simple peasants—anything to get the job done!

Fort Pierce also played host to the first Naval Combat Demolition Unit *(NCDU)*, training under the auspices of Lt Commander Draper D. Kaufman. Draper became known as the "father of demolition," and his career was stellar; he retired as a Rear Admiral in June 1973.

Ultimately, thirty-four units were trained for Operation Overlord, which was to become the most significant amphibious operation in World War II, D-Day, and the assault on France at the beaches of Normandy. It was at Normandy that now Lt (jg) Phil Bucklew USNR again distinguished himself and the U.S. Navy's special operations team. Lt Bucklew was in a lead Landing Craft Tank *(LCT)* in the first wave approaching Omaha Beach and was supposed to drop the ramp of the specialized vessel, which was carrying landing craft to allow Army tanks to go ashore and pave the way for the assault troops just three minutes behind. A mile from the shoreline he discovered that they were at the wrong disembarkation point, and the sea state was too rough for the tanks. He turned his *LCT* toward the correct beach location and proceeded with his passenger tanks and every other gun that could bear firing on beach targets. Just moments before the scheduled landing, twenty-eight tanks treadled forward onto the beach and began destroying German defenses. The landings quickly followed. Navy Reserve Lt (jg) Bucklew had earned another Navy Cross and a place in American naval history.

Normandy also was the site of a Presidential Unit Citation for the Navy Combat Demolition Unit (*NCDU*) of Force "Q" at Omaha Beach. Also won was a Navy Unit Commendation by the *NCDU* of Assault Force "U." These two awards represented two out of four given for U.S. Naval actions on D-Day. The casualty rate for these men was high at 52%. Omaha beach proved to be a tough nut to crack, and 32 *NCDU* men were killed and 63 wounded. Utah Beach experienced 2 killed and 16 wounded. The fierce determination of this new breed of navy fighting men did not go unnoticed. They paved the way for the beach assaults and the future of today's U.S. Navy Special Warfare. They were used extensively in the landings at Sicily, Salerno, southern France, and of course, Normandy. The Pacific Theater was not ignored, and six *NCDUs* served with General MacArthur's forces in his drive to retake the Philippine Islands. However, the assault on southern France marked the end of the *NCDU* due to organizational changes, and in reality began an evolution into something new. The *NCDUs* had performed beyond all expectations, and their role was developed into a different type of operation to meet specific or specialized needs. In the Pacific Theater of operations their role was changed, and the element of underwater work was added.

The predecessor to the Central Intelligence Agency (*CIA*) was the Office of Strategic Services (*OSS*), and *OSS* utilized what would ultimately become the SEALs for covert operations. In November 1943 the British Royal Navy (Combined Operations Specialist Lt Commander Wooley, RN) began training for operational swimmers of the OSS Maritime Group for work in the Pacific. The initial site was Camp Pendleton, just north of San Diego, California. They quickly relocated to Catalina Island, and then to the warmer waters off the Bahamas. British innovations such as the flexible fin (*Churchill fin*) were introduced, which enabled candidates to swim greater distances with far less fatigue. Limpet mines for destroying enemy vessels, re-breathing equipment, and submersibles (*sleeping beauty*—one man torpedoes) were also employed and improved by American personnel. What had been a European standard of specialized underwater warfare had come to the United States Navy.

The *OSS* trained underwater divers for specific missions, and when the Navy became more fully aware of their capabilities, it was only a short time before they were selected for amphibious preparatory duties, which included clearing beaches for landings. The difficulties and high casualties at the Tarawa landing in 1943 convinced the navy that success in amphibious operations dictated the use of advance specialized reconnaissance and removal of obstructions prior to landing troops.

Early in 1944 one hundred and eighty men, including 30 officers, were transferred to the Waimanalo Amphibious Training Facility on Oahu for advanced training in demolition. Underwater Demolition Teams (*UDT*) emerged from this early beginning and the knowledge gained from the *OSS* Maritime Group. *UDTs* One and Two were made up from this first group of 30 officers and 150 enlisted men, and they were assigned missions shortly after they were formed. Kwajalein and *Operation Flintlock* (the invasion of the Marshall Islands) became their baptism of fire. *UDTs* under the command of Lt Commander John T Koehler USNR inspected the beaches using drone boats that inexplicably ran wild. However, his swimmers were undaunted and returned with the information the landing force commander needed. As a result, the landing went off in an orderly fashion (Roi and Namur).

From this point forward until the end of World War II, the *UDTs*—or "waterborne commando," as Admiral Eric T Olson

World War II era UDT demolition experts demonstrate how they dismantled beach obstacles in the pre-invasion phase of an amphibious operation. Here they are using satchel charges loaded with explosives to blow up concrete and steel obstacles that would surely tear out the bottoms of fragile landing craft during an invasion. Their work was dangerous and required excellent swimming abilities, endurance, and good judgment. Author's Collection

has called them some 56 years later—became an indispensable part of amphibious warfare. Thirty-four *UDT* teams were formed during the last months of the war and fought their way to the shores of Japan. They had over 1,000 "frogmen" ready for the invasion of the Japanese home islands, but the war ended for them in their final operation at Balikpapan, Borneo, on July 4, 1945. This area had been a place where the Allies fled the Japanese onslaught three years before, and the *UDT's* were the first to return.

It is said that a *UDT* member received a surrender sword in Tokyo but was ordered by MacArthur to return it. After the war ended demobilization hit the new organization hard, and eventually there were only two teams on each coast of the USA. *UDT* Teams One and Three were assigned to Coronado, California, and Teams Two and Four to Little Creek, Virginia. The *UDT* staff at Coronado spent time writing a book of tactics for their operations that formed the basis for written doctrine in the future.

Each team was comprised of seven officers and forty enlisted men. The teams were poorly funded by the Navy and often had to purchase equipment with personal out of pocket money. They would have five years to wait for their services to be needed again. In June 1950, North Korean armed forces swept over South Korea, and the United States, as part of the newly formed United Nations, responded.

Korea, Vietnam, and the Cold War—SEALs & Combat Crew are Formalized

The bombing of the Japanese cities Nagasaki and Hiroshima with Atomic weapons and the relentless pounding by naval aircraft from aircraft carriers offshore convinced a war weary Emperor that enough was enough. He and his government agreed to unconditional surrender, and World War II drew to a close.

The end of World War II abruptly halted a process that was evolving into the creation of a military force with the combined skills that we know as modern day SEALs and Combat Crew. From one source or another demolition experts had joined with combat swimmers, who in turn had reconnaissance and other specialized skills. Add in the men who operated small boats in close proximity to enemy coastlines and submarine insertion and extraction, and the genesis of the SEALs and Combat Crew was evident. Despite the fact that the Cold War was already beginning with the Soviet Union and Soviet bloc nations, five years elapsed before the U.S. military was again involved in a shooting war. On June 25, 1950, North Korean regular army troops poured across the border into South Korea, and the Korean War began.

There was very little in the way of naval resources available to harass the advancing enemy, but U.S. and British aircraft carriers, as well as other warships, acted upon United

The *USS Carpellotti APD-136* in a rare color image of this high-speed troop transport. Although she operated off the east coast of the United States and was too late to see service in World War II, the *Carpellotti* was a prime example of the type of destroyer escort conversions to fast transport that UDT teams used in the Pacific War, Korea, and even in the Vietnam conflict. Author's Collection

One of the most famous images to come out of the Korean War was the demolition of harbor installations at Hungnam. The high-speed transport *USS Begor APD-127* has a front row seat for one of the war's largest explosions. The Hungnam Evacuation was an amphibious operation in reverse and lasted for two weeks, ending on Christmas Eve, 1950, with explosives set and ignited by UDT personnel. This denied the port and remaining assets to incoming North Korean armed forces. The UDT Teams waited for remaining stragglers, and all escaped on the last ship out, the *USS Catamount LSD-17*. The *Begor* landed UDT and British Commandos behind enemy lines to harass North Korean lines of communication and supply. Author's Collection

Nations authority and began to pound North Korean armed forces with everything at their disposal. It was not long before the *UDT* teams, or "frogmen," as they were called, were brought back into action.

At first, there were only eleven trained men available in *UDT* Team 3, but this number swelled to over 300 in three teams. Demolition and reconnaissance skills were vital to diffuse the Russian manufactured mines used by the North Koreans. Throughout the war it was estimated that over 4,000 contact and magnetic mines were laid, many of which were located and disposed of by *UDT* swimmers. The North Koreans became quite adept at sewing mines in and around harbors, and from the outset of the Korean conflict destroyers and minesweepers suffered greatly. Within months of the war's beginning, the minesweepers *USS Pledge AM-277* and *USS Pirate AM-275* were lost on a single day, October 12, 1950. *UDT* swimmers had been marking the location of mines, but had not been able to finish before the two minesweepers were fatally hit. *UDT* swimmers were able to rescue 25 men who would have been lost. Even before this action, *UDT* swimmers had been active at Inchon, marking and clearing mines and other obstructions in support of the astonishingly successful landings made by General MacArthur's forces behind

An obstruction is blown up by a SEAL team in preparation for an operation. Aside from destroying mines and clearing obstructions, SEALs routinely patrolled in the Mekong Delta area and other areas known to be infested with Viet Cong and North Vietnamese sympathizers. The SEAL teams worked closely with the CIA, other Special Forces, and the Brown Water Navy. U.S.N.I.

This is a picture of a badly damaged Riverine craft. This *ASPB (Assault Support Patrol Boat)* was holed at least three times, and the result was six dead—a "bad day." Many Riverine craft were damaged and sunk by a determined enemy working on his own home ground. The Brown Water Navy fought bravely in some of the most ferocious firefights in the Vietnam War. The following morning often showed the results, both in casualties and overall damage. Fiberglass, wood, and aluminum are not the best defense against rockets and shells. Author's Collection

This is a picture of the memorial to the Riverine Forces that served in Vietnam at the U.S. Naval Amphibious Base on Coronado Island, California. To the right is a *Swift Boat*, and in dark green a *PBR*, or fiberglass river patrol boat. The *PBRs* symbolized the Riverine Forces, and were designed specifically for the work in Vietnam. Author's Collection

the North Korean lines on September 15, 1950. Mine clearing was augmented with marking channels, crawling through mud flats, clearing fouled propellers, and acting as guides for landing craft. In essence, the *UDT* teams were performing the same tasks they became famous for in World War II, but in much colder water.

Aside from "up close and personal" minesweeping, the teams, as part of Special Operations Groups *(SOG)*, participated in raids on shore targets. Most popular were transportation systems, such as trains, tunnels, and bridges. The North Koreans transported much of their supplies and troops on the coastal routes, and *UDTs* became expert in derailing this system. Occasionally, personnel fluent in Russian would don a Russian army officer's uniform and go ashore from submarines or fast transports *(APD)* to mingle with North Koreans and gather intelligence.

The fast attack transports *(APD)* had been widely used during World War II in the Pacific, beginning with converted four piper/flush deck destroyers of World War I vintage that had been modified to carry four landing craft. These and other expendable vessels ferried everything from gasoline to *UDT* teams to points off shore, and then returned when a mission was completed. Toward the end of World War II, destroyer escorts under construction were converted for use as *APDs*. This was in response to the needs of amphibious commanders for a fast craft that could be used for reconnaissance, nuisance raids, channel marking, and obstacle identification or destruction. Converted destroyer escorts were again utilized in the Korean War. Some of the ships called back into service were the *USS Weiss APD-135, USS Horace Bass APD-124,* and *USS Diachenko APD-123*.

Submarines also played a role in the Korean War that was similar to the one played in World War II. On dark nights, converted submarines like the *USS Perch ASSP-313* would surface and launch commandos to raid North Korean shore

This is a picture of the "bull frog" trophy at the U.S. Navy Special Warfare Center in Coronado, California. This award goes to the SEAL who has served the longest active duty, and included 73-year-old SEAL Rudy Boesch (SEAL Team Two) of network television *"Survivor"* fame. Another celebrity SEAL is the flamboyant Governor Jesse Ventura of Minnesota. He served during the Vietnam War and is a favorite among SEAL Teams. Author's Collection

The "monster from the black lagoon" stands abreast of the "grinder," where neophyte SEAL candidates begin their journey. The statue was a gift from one of the SEAL classes and demonstrates that SEALs are not without a sense of humor. Author's Collection

installations. Of particular value was the disruption of supply trains that ran nightly up and down the Korean coastal routes.

UDT teams were assigned tasks, such as beach reconnaissance, capturing enemy officers for interrogation, and destroying the infrastructure of the North Korean coastline, including its fishing industry.

The Korean War ended in 1953, but activity in the Asian theater did not. Communist aggression seemed to be everywhere, and began to threaten an area only known as Indochina to most people. In actuality, it was in Vietnam that guerilla warfare became overwhelmingly apparent. During the late 1950s and early 1960s an insurgent group known as the Viet Cong began to undermine U.S. supported South Vietnam. The Viet Cong was backed by North Vietnam, China, and ultimately, the Soviet Union. Their avowed purpose was to reunite both countries into one nation ruled by a Communist government.

After the Korean War ended the *UDT* teams again had difficulty securing operating funds from the Navy Department, and just like post World War II again had to purchase vital

equipment (dive masks, air tanks) with their own salaries. Needed logistics and support vessels were virtually nonexistent. There was even some effort in the Pentagon to disband the Teams entirely because they were outside the more traditional naval establishment. Fortunately for the U.S. Navy, and the armed forces in general, this did not come to pass. But it was in this environment that Admiral Arleigh Burke, then Chief of Naval Operations, and many of his staff spoke of the need for a formalized counter guerilla force. Similarly, President John F Kennedy, who understood and appreciated fighting an enemy with unconventional means (he was a former *PT Boat* captain in the South Pacific), coined the concept of the SEALs. The U.S. Navy quickly obliged Kennedy's wishes, and in January 1962 SEAL Teams One and Two were established. SEAL Team One was designated for operations in Asia and South America, and SEAL Team Two was to deploy to Europe and Africa. This could be changed, however, dependent on operational needs.

The new designation **SEAL** was given to those who had been trained and experienced in the *UDT* teams. The mis-

This is a picture of a *Mark V* SEAL insertion/extraction craft that is manned and operated by Combat Crew. The *Mark V Special Operations Craft (SOC)* weighs fifty-seven tons, is 82' in length, and can make over 50 knots. It is one of the most versatile craft employed by the SEALs, and can be deployed anywhere in the world within 48 hours. It has state of the art electronics, and aside from weapons brought by the SEALs, its Combat Crew has twin and single fifty caliber machine guns and their own arsenal of personal weapons. Shown here is a *Mark V* leaving Coronado (rubber raft on the stern) for a training mission in January 2001. Author's Collection

sion was simple: successfully conduct secret counter guerilla operations in riverine and maritime environments. From this point, the SEALs and Riverine Forces that manned the River Patrol Boats, Swift Boats, and other inland water craft began to carve out a legend of not only courage, but cunning and wisdom in their war against the Viet Cong and Communism.

UDT teams still worked with amphibious groups during the seemingly endless series of battles that took place in the rivers and deltas that marked the lowland of South Vietnam. They acted as advisors and helped the South Vietnamese armed forces resist North Vietnamese aggression.

The Riverine Forces later evolved into the Special Combat Crew of today. In one operation after another they piloted fiberglass and aluminum boats at high speeds through some of the most treacherous inland waterways in South Vietnam. Most worked with Central Intelligence Agency operatives and had their bases of operations aboard converted *LSTs (USS Washtenaw County LST –1166)* and Barracks Ships, such as the *USS Benewah APB-35*. Early special boat operations doctrine was pioneered by boat crews operating from these ships moored in the brown waters of South Vietnamese rivers. From this the term "Brown Water" navy emerged. Even

some of the high-speed transports, such as the *USS Weiss APD-135*, were re-treaded for service in Vietnam and the UDT teams. In February 1964 Support Unit One of the "Brown Water" navy was inaugurated, and operated the fast torpedo boats and other craft to support Special Warfare operations. This was followed by other craft more suitable to the environment, such as the Swift Boats and famous 32' long fiberglass hull *PBRs* (river patrol boats). By the time the U.S. Navy began to turn over its responsibility to the South Vietnamese Navy in 1969 under the "Vietnamization Program," hundreds of craft were operating in the 7,000 square miles of swamps and deltas in South Vietnam. Unfortunately, most were captured when the North Vietnamese Army overran Saigon in 1975.

Vietnam was an unconventional war and honed the skills of what are now today the Combat Crew and the SEALs. The war wound down by the mid 1970s, and on May 1, 1983, all of the *UDT* teams were absorbed into the SEALs, as well as the fledgling swimmer delivery vehicles (*SDVs*).

The U.S. Naval Special Warfare Command was formally inaugurated in 1987 to encompass the SEAL Teams, *SDV* operations, Special Boat Units (*SBU*), and what became Combat Crew.

This picture is of the entrance to the UDT-SEAL Museum in Fort Pierce, Florida. The museum is acknowledged as the home of Naval Combat Demolition Units and is an excellent resource for those who want to trace the heritage of the UDT – NCDU – SEALs and Combat Crew. The museum also provides a little known but important service to the public at large by exposing fraudulent UDT and SEALs. The Special Warfare Community is tight knit and takes a very poor view of those who lie about being a member. UDT-SEAL Museum

Heritage of the United States Special Operations Command (USSOCOM)

The United States military establishment needed a specialized and rapid response force available for low intensity conflict, such as localized ethnic cleansing, counterterrorism, counter insurgency, and other minor work to moderate trouble spots in the world. Deploying a carrier battle group, a fully equipped Army Division, or even a Marine Amphibious Readiness Group in response to the sites where American or Allied interests were being threatened had proven to be a less than effective use of resources, as well as an over-extension of political and military power. While a carrier battle group or amphibious readiness group provides political leadership with undeniable clout, the unconventional wars in the early 21st century will rely greatly on units assigned to USSOCOM.

The lessons learned from the Invasion of Grenada in 1983 spoke volumes about lack of coordination and cooperation among Special Operations and conventional military forces. It further demonstrated that the interrelationship between specially trained organizations that are mission specific and traditional "big" Navy, Army, and Air Force units was unacceptable. The result was the proverbial use of a battleship to sink a rowboat and unusually high casualties among the nation's best fighting forces. October 1983 also witnessed

This is an image of the original frogman, or UDT swimmer, statue at the UDT-SEAL Museum in Fort Pierce, Florida. This is what was called the "naked warrior" of World War II, and now the SEAL of the 21st Century. UDT – SEAL Museum

This is the logo for the United States Special Operations Command, which includes the Joint Operations Command, Airborne, Air Force Special Operations Command, and the United States Navy Special Warfare Command. USSOCOM is a specially funded operation that carries out a variety of functions not readily suitable for the mainstream armed forces. The motto of USSOCOM is "The Quiet Professionals." U.S. Navy

the death of 237 Marines at the hands of a terrorist bomber in Lebanon. Even prior to the difficulties encountered during the Grenada operation, the U.S. military suffered casualties during an abortive attempt to rescue 53 hostages being held by Iranian extremists. The mission to rescue American citizens being held was a failure and marked a low point for coordinated U.S. Military operations. Something had to be done to enhance American small operations capability to restore confidence in the power of U.S. armed forces worldwide. October 1983 clearly marked the watershed of special operations; a new concept had to be inaugurated, and above all, supported by the military establishment and civilian leadership.

Congressional reviews in the United States Senate and House of Representatives were carried out in the years that followed the Grenada invasion. In essence, Special Operations *needed a seat at the military decision making table* and the resources to carry out their tasks without wholesale interference by the entrenched military hierarchy. The congressional investigations led to the Goldwater-Nichols Defense Reorganization Act of 1986. Implementation of the elements of this act was difficult in light of Pentagon opposition and that of the Reagan White House. It took a further amendment (1987) in the form of the Nunn-Cohen Act, brought about by then Senator Sam Nunn and Senator (later Department of Defense Secretary) William Cohen) to add teeth and cohesiveness to the concept of Special Operations Forces. This change in organizational structure was a double edged sword, as the new organization had to achieve its objectives without openly alienating the armed forces it sought to enhance and interact with.

President Ronald Reagan ultimately approved the formation of a new military establishment on April 13, 1987, and the Department of Defense activated the United States Special Operations Command *(USSOCOM)* on April 16, 1987.

The new command was entitled to have a civilian deputy in the Department of Defense, a four star general in command, and very importantly, a Major Force Program (11) budget that was to be expended solely on special operations. This became known as the *SOF* "checkbook," and provided the financial independence required to provide advanced weaponry and other support to the units within the command. Ironically, the entire *USSOCOM* budget is only about 1% of the Department of Defense's annual grant from congress. It was further agreed that units that became part of Special Operations would also become tenants at respective military installations, and thus fully responsible for the building and upkeep of their facilities. For example, U.S. Navy Special Warfare would be treated as a tenant on any naval installation it occupied or occupies.

At first **USSOCOM** was comprised of **75ᵗʰ Army Ranger Regiment, 1ˢᵗ, 5ᵗʰ, and 10ᵗʰ Special Forces Groups (airborne), 160ᵗʰ Special Operations Aviation Regiment (airborne),** and a variety of **Reserve** and **National Guard Units**. Also included were the **John F Kennedy Special Warfare Center,** the **4ᵗʰ Psychological Operations Group (PSYOPS)**, and the **96ᵗʰ Civil Affairs Operation**. The U.S. Navy's contribution was the newly crated **Naval Special Warfare Command Center**, a training only facility.

It was a rocky beginning, but a beginning nonetheless. At this point *USSOCOM* was virtually all Army, with a small naval training center. Regardless of organizational structure it was clear from the outset that if Special Operations was going to be successful they must have the ability to mobilize and travel at a moment's notice, and this meant on land, sea, and in air. Direct access to assets that could transport forces was an absolute necessity.

During this time the U.S. Air Force operated the 23ʳᵈ Air Force, which had the dual roles of providing airlift support to

This is an AC-130 Spectre gunship. which is one of the variants of the old standby C-130 aircraft. The AC-130 Spectre is assigned to the Air Force Special Operations Command and is utilized for close air support, interdiction and armed reconnaissance, drop and extraction zone defense, and combat search and rescue. These are heavily armed with side firing weapons that are tied to sensors that allow surgical strike or saturation firepower. The Spectres house some of the most reliable and sensitive electronic equipment, and are able to pierce the darkness or inclement weather and hunt down enemy forces while excluding friendly troops. The Spectre is an excellent adjunct to Naval Special Warfare. USAF

Special Forces and military airlift capability of other elements of the U.S. armed forces. *USSOCOM* required a dedicated airlift and support command, and on May 22, 1990, after prolonged negotiations, the 23rd Air Force relegated its other duties to other commands in the Air Force and became the **Air Force Special Operations Command**. At an earlier date, the U.S. Navy made its own sacrifice to *USSOCOM*.

The U.S. Navy wanted to retain Naval Special Warfare Groups I and II, which included the SEALs and Special Boat Units; in other words, the fighting component. It was reasoned that these Groups were a necessary part of the Pacific and Atlantic Fleets and should remain under naval leadership.

Argument and debate was heated in the Pentagon over this issue, and finally *USSOCOM* won out. On October 1, 1988, all of U.S. **Navy Special Warfare** passed into the administration of Special Operations. Special Operations now provides 95% of the budget for Naval Special Warfare, and the remaining 5% is from the Navy Department. The overall budget allotment for Naval Special Warfare represents about 17% of *USSOCOM* funding.

By late 1990 the Special Operations Command based out of MacDill Air Force Base in Tampa, Florida, was intact, and began the process of integrating its diversity of forces, which now consisted of Army Rangers, Army Special Forces, Navy SEALs and Combat Crew, Air Force Special Operations, and a host of other units. There was no representation in *USSOCOM* by the Marine Corps, which preferred to maintain a separate force in the form of *Marine Recon* (reconnaissance) as a necessary component of their amphibious capability.

The U.S. Navy Special Warfare Command now had a dual relationship with the U.S. Navy; however, it derived its primary support and command direction from *USSOCOM*. What had been strongly opposed at a number of levels of

Another element of the U.S. Special Operations Command is the *75th Ranger Regiment*, shown here at its activation of headquarters and battalion levels on October 3, 1984. Here the distinguished regiment receives its colors amid the good will of the Korean War era Rangers. On February 3, 1986, World War II and Korean War colors were consolidated and now belong to *USSOCOM*. U.S. Army

government and in the backrooms of politics had come to fruition.

The SEALs and Combat Crew have a distinguished pedigree earned in the heat of battle. They are taught to be courageous but wise, strong but clever, and above all act as a unit rather than as individuals. They carry out their missions and they take care of their own. **"I will do nothing to dishonor my unit, my navy, or my country."** These are not just words, they form the credo of a very special group of dedicated men.

Chapter 2

Overview of SEALs and Combat Crew

The SEALs and Combat Crew are selected not for brawn and braggadocio, but for cunning, intelligence, endurance, and allegiance to their code and team. They, in their own words, are "*not your average bears*." They are also nothing like they are portrayed in feature films or tabloid magazine articles. The Special Warfare Community is a highly trained, combat focused, and motivated group of individuals that have evolved from World War II, Korean, and Vietnam War Scouts and Raiders, Underwater Demolition Teams, Naval Combat Demolition Units, and Riverine (Brown Water Navy) forces. Modern day SEALs and Combat Crew have incorporated all of the skills of their ancestors, and have added many new skills. They have also improved weapons and equipment, especially in the area of electronics. These things, plus a proven division of labor, contribute to the overall success of

the U.S. Navy Special Warfare Command. This is particularly impressive given the short time from their formal creation in 1987. The command is continually evolving into a weapons force that can meet and defeat any other military force in the world. When belligerent armed forces are confronted with the possibility that the U.S. may employ SEAL teams or their allies, the complexion of the battle changes significantly. SEALs and Combat Crew are world renowned for success, having proven themselves in many situations.

Organizational Sturcture of the U.S. Navy Special Warfare Command

The command reports to the Commander, U.S. Special Operations Command (*USSOCOM*), and maintains a cooperative/advisory relationship with the Chief of Naval Operations

The Naval Amphibious Base in Coronado, California. Generations of *UDT* and SEAL teams have passed through this base, which has access to San Diego Bay on its east perimeter and the Pacific Ocean on the Silver Strand Beach. It is ironic for SEAL candidates to be smashing through the surf or panting during a jog just yards away from the world famous Hotel Del Coronado. Hotel regulars have become accustomed to naval operations and pay little attention. Author's Collection

SEAL trainees carrying their inflatable boat to the surf, where they will paddle past the surf line and return. The anguish in their faces tells it all—to be a SEAL requires commitment and endurance to the limit of human capability. U.S. Navy

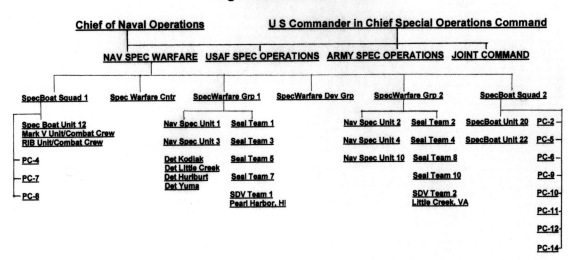

U S Navy Special Warfare Command
Organizational Structure

Chief of Naval Operations   **U S Commander in Chief Special Operations Command**

NAV SPEC WARFARE   **USAF SPEC OPERATIONS**   **ARMY SPEC OPERATIONS**   **JOINT COMMAND**

SpecBoat Squad 1   **Spec Warfare Cntr**   **SpecWarfare Grp 1**   **SpecWarfare Dev Grp**   **SpecWarfare Grp 2**   **SpecBoat Squad 2**

Spec Boat Unit 12	**Nav Spec Unit 1**	**Seal Team 1**	**Nav Spec Unit 2**	**Seal Team 2**	**SpecBoat Unit 20**	**PC-2**

Spec Boat Unit 12
Mark V Unit/Combat Crew
RIB Unit/Combat Crew

- PC-4
- PC-7
- PC-8

Nav Spec Unit 1 — **Seal Team 1**
Nav Spec Unit 3 — **Seal Team 3**

Det Kodiak — **Seal Team 5**
Det Little Creek
Det Hurlburt — **Seal Team 7**
Det Yuma

SDV Team 1
Pearl Harbor, HI

Nav Spec Unit 2 — **Seal Team 2**
Nav Spec Unit 4 — **Seal Team 4**
Nav Spec Unit 10 — **Seal Team 8**

Seal Team 10

SDV Team 2
Little Creek, VA

SpecBoat Unit 20 — **PC-2**
SpecBoat Unit 22 — **PC-5**
— **PC-6**
— **PC-9**
— **PC-10**
— **PC-11**
— **PC-12**
— **PC-14**

Notes:

Special Boat Squadron One, Naval Special Warfare Center & Naval Special Warfare Group One are headquartered in Coronado, California / Flag Officer, U S Naval Special Warfare headquartered in Coronado. Seal Teams 7 & 10 commissioned in 2001.

Special Boat Squadron Two, Naval Special Warfare Group Two & Development Group are headquartered in Little Creek, VA

Nav Spec Unit 1(Guam); Nav Spec Unit 2(Stuttgart, Germany); Nav Spec Unit 3(Bahrain); Nav Spec Unit 4(Roosevelt Roads, PR); Nav Spec Unit 10(Rota Spain). There are small-specialized detachments located at Kodiak, AK.; Little Creek, VA.; Hurlburt, FL. & Yuma, AR.

SDV – Seal Delivery Vehicle
PC - Cyclone class coastal patrol craft (PC's 3, 9, 10, 11 tentatively scheduled for decommissioning over the next three years) / Mark V – Special Operations Craft (SOC) / RIB – Rigid Inflatable Boat

Organizational chart of U.S. Navy Special Warfare and its relationship to USSOCOM, headquartered in Tampa, Florida.

U S NAVY SPECIAL WARFARE COMMAND
(Base of Operations)
SEAL TEAM ASSIGNED AREAS OF OPERATIONS

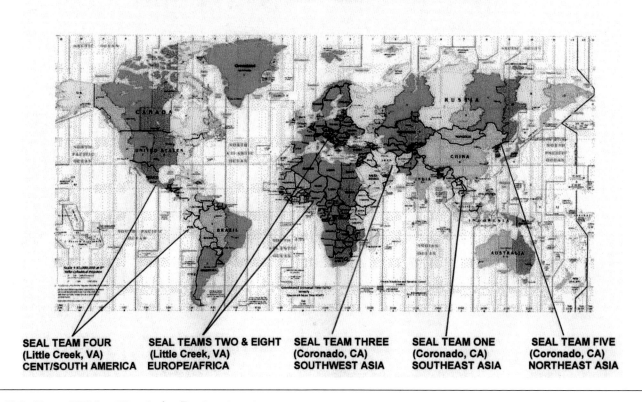

SEAL TEAM FOUR
(Little Creek, VA)
CENT/SOUTH AMERICA

SEAL TEAMS TWO & EIGHT
(Little Creek, VA)
EUROPE/AFRICA

SEAL TEAM THREE
(Coronado, CA)
SOUTHWEST ASIA

SEAL TEAM ONE
(Coronado, CA)
SOUTHEAST ASIA

SEAL TEAM FIVE
(Coronado, CA)
NORTHEAST ASIA

(*CNO*). The Command is one of the four major components in American naval forces, along with Aviation, Surface Warfare, and Submarines.

U.S. Navy Special Warfare is under the command of a Rear Admiral (SEAL) who flies his flag at the Special Warfare Center in Coronado, California, in conjunction with the Naval Amphibious Base. The Command is divided into six major components:

- Special Boat Squadron One, which is based at Coronado, California, and includes Special Boat Unit 12 (*Mark V* and *Rigid Hulled Inflatable Boats (RIB)*, and Patrol Gunboats *USS Monsoon PC-4, USS Squall PC-7, USS Hurricane PC-*3, and *USS Zephyr PC-8*).
- Special Warfare Center – headquarters U.S. Navy Special Warfare based in Coronado, California.
- Special Warfare Group One includes: SEAL Teams 1, 3, 5, 7* based out of Coronado, California; Naval Special Units One (Guam) and Three (Bahrain), as well as detachments in Kodiak, Alaska, Little Creek, Virginia, Hurlburt, Florida, and Yuma, Arizona, which are also based out of Coronado, California; and Seal delivery Vehicle (SDV) One, which is based out of Pearl Harbor, Hawaii.
- Special Warfare Development Group, which is a "think tank" for analysis and development of new weapons, systems, counter terrorism, and techniques for Navy Special Warfare. This center is based at the East Coast Naval Amphibious Facility.
- Special Warfare Group Two includes: SEAL Teams 2, 4, 8, and 10* based out of Little Creek, Virginia; and Naval Special Units Two (Germany), Four (Puerto Rico), and Ten (Spain), as well as SEAL Delivery Vehicle (*SDV*) Team 2, which are also based at Little Creek, Virginia.
- Special Boat Squadron Two includes Special Boat Units 20 & 22, as well as patrol gunboats: *USS Tempest PC-2*; *USS Typhoon PC-5*; *USS Sirocco PC-6*; *USS Chinook PC-9**; *USS Firebolt PC-10**; *USS Whirlwind PC-11**; *USS Thunderbolt PC-12*; and *USS Tornado PC-14.*

* SEAL Teams Seven and Ten were established in 2001, and patrol gunboats *Hurricane, Chinook, Firebolt*, and *Whirlwind* were scheduled to be decommissioned in 2002. However, the emphasis on homeland defense has meant these craft will be used in harbor defense. The namesake of the coastal patrol ship (PC) *USS Cyclone PC-1* was transferred to the U.S. Coast Guard in February 2000 for use in the suppression of illegal drugs. The *PCs* are excellent platforms for this type of operation.

This is the current and projected organization of U.S. Navy Special Warfare Command, however, this can change with wartime augmentations and the introduction of new weap-

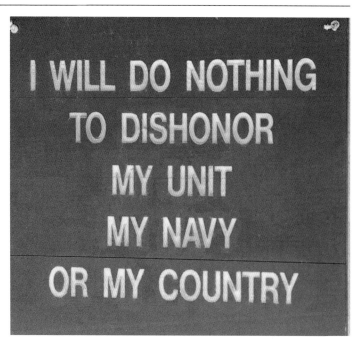

The code of the SEALs: *"I WILL DO NOTHING TO DISHONOR MY UNIT, MY NAVY, OR MY COUNTRY."* This is located near the "grinder," where candidates gather for instruction and daily assignments at the Naval Special Warfare Training Center in Coronado, California. Author's Collection

ons systems, such as the Advanced SEAL Delivery System (*ASDS*), a mini dry submersible.

The Command is composed of approximately 4,950 active personnel and 1,200 reservists. Of the active personnel, 850 are officers, and there are over 4,100 enlisted. There are 400 SEAL officers and 400 officers who are not SEALs. Of the enlisted personnel, 2,100 are SEALs or SEAL qualified, and slightly over 500 are Combat Crew. 1,500 are support

A helo (helicopter) drops SEALs on the deck of an aircraft carrier during a mock exercise. Realism, training, and more training hone the skills of the SEALs and Combat Crew. This is especially vital, as many of the Naval Special Warfare Community have not been exposed to combat such as that in Vietnam. U.S. Navy

Opposite: SEAL team operating areas of responsibility on a worldwide basis. It is significant that *USSOCOM* brought two new SEAL teams on line in 2001 to realign the current force. One team from each coast will deploy for six month periods. Trouble spots in maritime environments worldwide seem to be proliferating. Author's Collection

A contingent of SEALs approaches a target in Bosnia after being landed by helicopter. Although this is a training exercise, it is as real as the team can make it. The SEALs do not let up for a moment—there is too much at stake. U.S. Navy

staff, and over 200 are SEAL Delivery Vehicle or dry deck shelter qualified.

The reserve component of Naval Special Warfare (NSW) maintains their skills and physical fitness in order to be readily available for recall in a national emergency. They routinely train with active duty staff and keep abreast of new equipment and technology being introduced into special warfare. In the Naval Special Warfare community, there is *no such thing as an "ex– SEAL."*

The Coastal Patrol Gunboats (PC) are commanded and officered by Surface Warfare Officers, but the *Mark V* Special Operations Craft and the *RHIB* or *RIB* (rigid hull inflatable boat) are commanded by qualified Combat Crew.

Overall, U.S. Navy Special Warfare is housed primarily in Coronado, California, and Little Creek, Virginia. Both are historical sites for amphibious training, which goes hand in hand with SEAL and Combat Crew operations. Although Navy Special Warfare is primarily situated on the major coasts of the United States, its assets, including the *Mark V* boat, can respond to trouble spots world wide in 24-48 hours. In some

The namesake of the *Cyclone* class coastal patrol boats (PC), the *USS Cyclone PC-1*. The *Cyclone* was commissioned on August 7, 1993, and the last of her class, the *USS Tornado PC-14*, entered naval service on June 24, 2000. Intended as a vessel to provide a temporary home for SEALs as they carried out their missions in the littoral, the *Cyclone* class has had mixed reviews by its owners and operators—the Naval Special Warfare community. The 331-ton f/l vessels have a top speed of 35 knots and can cruise 2,000 nautical miles at 12 knots. They are not well adapted to heavy sea states, and provide more than a rough ride for their crews. Several of the units have been selected to be retrofitted for accommodating the easy recovery of an 11 meter Rigid Hulled Inflatable Boat (RIB). The *Cyclone* has been turned over to the U.S. Coast Guard for use in areas where drug smuggling at sea is prevalent. For this task, the fast, heavily armed *Cyclone* class is ideal. Other cyclone class PCs will be used in homeland defense. U.S. Navy

instances, the response time is even faster, depending on the assets available and location of the threat.

SEAL teams are composed of eight platoons, which in turn consist of two officers and fourteen enlisted men each. A Lieutenant generally commands the platoons, and if needed the platoons can be broken down into two squads of eight men each. The basis for this organizational structure rests on interlocking teamwork. With such a small group each man

The now-decommissioned 36-year-old *USS Kamehameha SSN-642*, a converted *Benjamin Franklin* nuclear ballistic missile submarine, as she enters Apra Harbor, Guam, on April 13, 2001. The former *SSBN-642* was converted to an attack submarine (*SSN*) in 1992, and served as a Special Warfare delivery vehicle. The *Kamehameha* is shown carrying its two dry-deck shelters (*DDS*) aft of the sail. The dry-deck shelters carry SEALs and contemporary SEAL Delivery Vehicles (*SDV*) to trouble spots around the globe. At this time, tensions between the U.S. and China were heightened due to the forced landing of a U.S. Navy *EP-3E* surveillance aircraft and its crew of 24 on Hainan Island off the Chinese coast. The aircraft crew was later freed through diplomatic efforts. U.S. Navy

Coronado, California: a Special Operations Craft (*SOC*) prepares for a training mission in late January 2001. These 57 ton craft are armed with twin and single .50 caliber machine guns, 7.62 machine guns, and 40 mm grenade launchers. The personal weapons of the Combat Crew and SEALs augment this arsenal. The *Mark V SOC* can carry sixteen SEALs at speeds exceeding 50 knots to their destination, and can launch swimmers or up to four Combat Rubber Raiding Craft (*CRRC*). Author's Collection

knows exactly what the other is capable of and where he will be at any given moment. Some of the men on a team are trained in one or more specialties, and each team member has varying degrees of skill, however, all are capable of carrying out a mission. Missions are planned in detail by SEAL team personnel and staff. SEALs rely on thorough preparation and planning with intelligent forethought. The "blood and guts" charge went out of vogue long before SEALs began carrying out special warfare operations.

A SEAL team platoon in concert with a RIB detachment of boats and Combat Crew routinely deploy with each Amphibious Ready Group (Navy/Marine Corps *ARG*), and remain with the group throughout its assignment. A SEAL platoon is assigned to each Carrier Battle Group in the Pacific, but remains ashore until needed. Conversely, a SEAL platoon embarks with each Carrier Battle Group (*CBG*) in the Atlantic. In any event, theater combat commanders have SEALs and portable boats at their disposal should the need arise.

U.S. Naval Special Warfare Missions

The SEALs and Combat Crew have a worldwide reach; thus, they can provide strategic as well as tactical value to the U.S. armed forces. *The world is their operating area*, and they can have an impact on up to 60% of the earth's people and industry. This 60% is within 60 miles of the ocean, and only forty-three countries are landlocked, as opposed to 148 countries that are approachable by water.

Since the decline and fall of the Soviet Union, littoral warfare and low intensity conflict have become prominent in the thinking of politicians, diplomats, and the military forces of most nations. This has necessitated the use of SEALs and Combat Crew in littorals, rivers, and maritime and coastal targets. This type of warfare or action is expected to increase with the United States being the sole super power. Until other nations develop their conventional naval foces to a level minimally commensurate with the U.S. Navy, unconventional warfare will be in the forefront of combat. For this USSOCOM and the SEALs are ideal.

Special warfare communities are growing internationally and our allies are of great assistance, but unfortunately our enemies and other potential belligerents have also taken up the cause of special warfare.

In general, U.S. Navy Special Warfare engages in the following mission arenas:

- Combating Terrorism through direct and indirect action. SEALs may be called upon to locate and dispose of terrorists (non-domestic), or locate them for friendly powers to take action. SEALs may be used covertly to retaliate against those terrorists that attacked U.S. soil on September 11, 2001. The terrorist attack and U.S. count operation define unconventional warfare.
- Special Reconnaissance for Naval or Special Operations Units. This would include a seaborne or airborne approach and no direct action surveillance.
- Direct Action – SEALs deployed to an area where an objective must be destroyed, secured, or a problem resolved through combat action.
- Foreign internal defense – providing a force that will augment friendly forces in defense of an ally.

Two Rigid Hulled Inflatable Boats *(RIB)* stand by at pierside in Coronado, California, prior to a training run in January 2001. The Naval Special Warfare *RIB* is 35 feet 11 inches (11 meters) in length, and the neoprene sponsons that surround all but the aft part of the boat are for seakeeping and spray reduction. This boat was designed with the input of the SEALs and Combat Crew and fits their needs far better than predecessor units. The boats have a crew of three and can carry a SEAL squad of eight men. These boats serve as an excellent means of insertion and extraction of special warfare personnel in hostile waters. Author's Collection

- Information Warfare, counter proliferation, psychological operations, and ultimately civil affairs to stabilize friendly governments and assure continued good will towards the United States.
- Unconventional warfare - when a carrier air strike, ship bombardment with missiles or gunfire, or amphibious landing is impractical, then the SEALs can be brought in to achieve mission results. This can include clearing beach obstacles, mines, and neutralizing enemy strong holds below the high water mark.

U.S. Navy Special Warfare is multi-purpose and highly flexible, and will likely play an increasing role by carrying out national policy abroad. Fortunately or unfortunately, the scope of their activities will be known to a few and rarely ever become public. These men make many personal sacrifices and perform bravely for their country, but when they return from a mission there is no hero's welcome waiting, because it is all classified. They must be content with the knowledge that they have performed a valuable service for their country and take pride in a job well done. How the SEALs and Combat Crew are trained speaks reams about what they do and will do in the future. The very fact that the United States government sustains the *USSOCOM* and its maritime combat component tells much about international conditions in the "new world order."

Chapter 3

Training - Earning the Trident

Among the pins and insignia worn by U.S. Navy personnel, the *Trident*, or Special Warfare Pin, is the most respected. Those who have earned it know what arduous training really is and how miserable life can be. It should be noted, however, that the training phases are just the beginning, and after an individual earns his Trident and is assigned to a SEAL Team, there is no let up. SEALs train, exercise, and mission plan throughout the balance of their careers. Once the Trident is pinned on the uniform of a SEAL he has to be worthy of it every day during his naval career in Special Warfare.

This training has become world renowned for the finely tuned combat professional it produces. Countries such as Bangladesh, South Korea, Peru, Singapore, Thailand, and Tunisia have enrolled candidates from their own armed forces for this training. Singapore leads with eight candidates during 1999-2000. This has produced a collateral benefit to American forces when they are called upon to carry out a mission in concert with or near these areas. A friendly face can cut through a lot of foreign red tape.

SEAL and/or Seal Delivery Vehicle Team members are trained in three identifiable courses:

- **Basic Underwater Demolition/SEAL (BUD/S)** – 25 weeks divided into three phases (Physical conditioning, Underwater training, and Land Warfare)
- **Jump School (Parachute Training) at Fort Benning** – Ranger and Green Beret Training center.
- **SEAL Qualification Training (SQT)** – 15 weeks of pre-SEAL team assignment (specialized skills, including weapons, tactics, communications, air operations, and combat swimming)

The Face of BUD/S. A sand and salt encrusted weary trainee reluctantly poses for a photograph at the U.S. Naval Special Warfare Center in Coronado, California. This SEAL candidate has just come out of the surf and rolled around in the sand as part of a training evolution to teach neophyte SEALs what it is really like to be sandy, dirty, cold, and wet. U.S. Navy

The infamous "grinder," where it all begins. Here class 232 is underway and out training. A lone sailor walks across the asphalt area that is marked with little "frogman" fins to indicate where a trainee is to stand, where successful and unsuccessful trainees have stood, and where others will stand in the future. Later, the graduation of the few remaining BUD/S trainees will also take place on the "grinder." Author's Collection

SEAL candidates lock arms in the surf and await the orders of their instructors. Contrary to films and tabloid magazines, SEAL instructors are not unduly cruel to trainees; the elements of water, dirt, mud, and cold contribute sufficient punishment. U.S. Navy

A look at the BUD/S training and obstacle course at the Naval Special Warfare Center. It is deserted now, and the weather is beautiful. Soon it will be crawling with men from the Naval Academy, OCS, and the enlisted ranks attempting to carry out one physical training evolution after another. The weather does not always cooperate so well, but BUD/S trainees work rain or shine. Author's Collection

SEAL training is unique in that it includes commissioned officers and enlisted men in the same course, and each must succeed on their own merit. No advantage is provided based on rate or rank. SEAL candidates come from the U.S. Naval Academy, Officers Candidate School, the Fleet, and Boot Camp. They are all volunteers. The candidates are thoroughly screened through background checks, and information is gathered about their abilities. They must be mature, intelligent, physically fit, and in excellent health. The physical training involved in SEAL training is generally considered to be the most brutal of any military training program. Candidates that have a regular workout program and run long distances

as part of their normal lifestyle have a definite edge to be accepted for training. The annual candidate pool is generally 600-800 men and includes over one third with a bachelor's degree. Often the number in a beginning class is 150 students. All are selected based on the severest of criteria, and intelligence is as equally important as physical strength. SEALs operate in small groups of sixteen, eight, or less, and teamwork and thinking on their feet prevent casualties.

Running long distances in ever-shorter periods of time and carrying increasing weight loads is a definite requirement for success as a SEAL candidate. Those that think they can be accepted need to know that swimming, bicycling, and

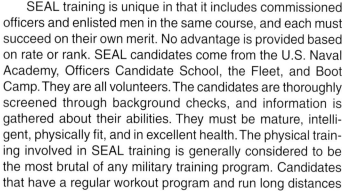

A class gathers for instruction and orders from Navy Special Warfare instructors who have all gone through what their charges are going through. In the background are combat relics, such as a helicopter carcass and an elderly landing craft that are used in training. Author's Collection

An old stand-by for instructors is to have the class do push-ups as part of a calculated program of calisthenics. Nearby is a canteen of water that the candidates are encouraged to use frequently. The average trainee drinks up to four quarts of fluid per day during BUD/S. Author's Collection

The tower that must be climbed without assistance or a ladder. Once atop the tower, the candidate must exit down one of the attached ropes. Instructors do not just say "get up there," but demonstrate the proper way of climbing, and then say, "get up there" or words to that affect. Author's Collection

Candidates that have successfully ascended to the top of the pole tower then descend using "slide for life" ropes. SEALs have to enter and exit areas in a variety of ways, and knowledge of the use of rope is critical. It is also a confidence tester. Author's Collection

weight lifting provide just so much in the way of preparation for what SEAL instructors demand of the candidates. Running is the key to success, as it strengthens the lower extremities of the body to the level required to endure SEAL training and the operations to come. Added to this is the ever increasing need to improve overall cardiovascular capability, and a diet high in complex carbohydrates helps a candidate to endure the rigors of training. Despite the fact that candidates are youthful (under 28 years of age) and think they are invincible, consumption of alcohol, smoking, and poor dietary habits will hinder and ultimately prevent a candidate from becoming a SEAL. Drug usage of any king other than that

prescribed and known to instructors is forbidden. The SEALs are not looking for steroid pumped muscle impaired giants.

In terms of physical preparation, a candidate that has not been regularly in a physical training plan should be able to run 16 miles (in boots) in four mile segments each week. After nine weeks of preparatory physical training (PT), a candidate should be able to perform a minimum of 80 pushups, 180 sit-ups, and 30 pull-ups. A candidate that has been regularly working out should be able to run 30 miles (in boots) in six-mile segments and perform 400 push-ups, 500 sit-ups, and 40 pull-ups. Of course, this regimen is not to be performed all at once, but in repetitions, with breaks between

Climbing the wall without assistance is a means to determine the fitness of each candidate. Scaling a building at night or climbing aboard a moored ship during a "ship takedown" requires this type of skill. Author's Collection

Simple bars or playground "monkey bars" develop upper body strength and the ability to hold on. Later, a SEAL may be carrying over 100 pounds of equipment and have to rely on his arms and upper body strength to save his life or that of his team. Author's Collection

Walking a rope bridge appears easy. Just try it some time and look out for the ground as you swing downward, or worse, if you lose both your footing and let go of the rope railings at the same time. Author's Collection

Scaling bars by going over and under is much more difficult than it looks, and as can be seen, trainees are doing it in timed fashion by a rather skeptical instructor. Author's Collection

each (e.g. 20 X 20 pushups). For any candidate who thinks they are up to this program, Basic Underwater Demolition/ SEAL, or BUD/S training, is where it all begins.

The First Step – BUD/S Training –
"Where the Average Bears Leave the Woods"

Basic Underwater Demolition/SEALs, or BUD/S training, is conducted at the Naval Special Warfare Training Center in Coronado, California. Like all specialized training programs, there are preliminaries that include highly selective screening, ensuring that the candidates meet all qualifications.

The training begins with a five-week Pre-BUD/S, or SEAL Indoctrination Program. This course is designed to prepare applicants for the rigors of BUD/S, and is physically inten-

As one trainee said, "the BUD/S program is far beyond my standard of physical training, and has not disappointed me yet." A trainee attempts to hopefully cover a distance by swinging from one ring to a rope and all over again. The physical training never ceases during BUD/S, except for classroom instruction sessions. Author's Collection

The 60-foot high cargo net, which requires a BUD/S trainee to climb up and back down again—over and over. On many occasions, the only way to scale the side of a hostile ship or waterborne platform is via an abandoned or unused cargo net or rope ladder. SEALs need to know that getting there can be more difficult than the mission itself, and must be prepared. Author's Collection

A broken down *"Chinook"* helicopter is located at the south end of the training compound for use by trainees. Thousands of trainees have tramped through this old chopper. Author's Collection

A reminder of the past. This steel hulled Landing Craft (Mechanized) *LCM* was developed in World War II, was used in the Korean Conflict, and was often modified for use by the Riverine Forces and SEALs in the Vietnam War. This land locked craft is still used by future SEALs as part of their training. Author's Collection

sive. The exercises in the SEAL Indoctrination are identical to those included in the Basic Underwater Demolition/SEAL training regimen. The indoctrination program is designed to weed out those candidates who would likely be unsuccessful in BUD/S training. The training of SEALs and Combat Crew is very expensive, and the goal is the successful training of those men who are selected. If an applicant is successful in demonstrating competence in indoctrination training they are selected for Basic Underwater Demolition (BUD/S) training. BUD/S training is divided into three phases:

- Phase I Orientation and Physical Training Phase
- Phase II Dive Phase
- Phase III Land Warfare Phase

BUD/S starts with a physically fit candidate and turns out graduates that are in absolute top condition. Phase I begins with the formation of a training class as identified by a number (e.g. 224, 234, and so forth). For those that make it through to their *Trident,* this is a number that will never be forgotten. Candidates are gathered in classrooms and on the "grinder," an open asphalt parade ground where they are given an ori-

The logs, and that which is most despised—"Old Misery." The 400- to 50-pound, 16-foot long logs are used by boat crews to improve their physical strength, but mainly to establish a rapport and develop a team that works together. Success as a SEAL is dependent on teamwork, and there is no room for spectators or showboating. "Old Misery" (to the left) is 100 pounds heavier, and is used for boat crews that are not quite up to speed as a team. The mere mention of this particular log is a great motivator. Author's Collection

Eight of the rubber boats used by crews to negotiate the surf, develop a team attitude, and ultimately come alongside and board a series of boulders that jet out into the surf on the beach. These boats are rugged and must be hauled up and over the rocks time and time again in an evolution known as "rock portage." Many a rib and other bones are injured or broken during this exercise. Author's Collection

Boat crews march out toward the surf with their boats overhead. During "hell week," some trainees claimed to have been able to sleep while walking with a boat attached to their head. Inside the boat are the wooden oars used for propulsion, and each candidate must wear a life vest for safety. U.S. Navy

BUD/S Trainees cross the street at a jog to head for the beach and a run. Each is carrying a heavy load, and the pace never stops. Like the author, occasionally a mother or grandmother stands at this spot to take a photograph of their son or grandson. For a BUD/S trainee, this can be comparable to a date with "old misery." Author's Collection

entation as to what will be expected, and the means to carry out their upcoming assignments. In the main, they will be taught to act as a team. There are no star quarterbacks here. Each man helps the other, or it will not work for the team. This first lesson is taught through the use of small rubber boats and telephone poles or logs (one of which is known as "old misery"). "Old Misery" is 100 pounds heavier than the other logs and is used as a motivational tool for those boat crews that need encouragement in the form of additional work and pain. The teams will lift and hold the logs aloft until told to lay them down or shift them to another position. This is an impossible task without maximum effort from each person. These exercises definitely help the trainees to understand that one man cannot fail his team.

The black and yellow striped boats that hold up to six trainees are also a common sight on the Silver Strand Beach, and daily, applicants must take their boats out through the surf, time and time again, to master surf line operations. Coming ashore and leaving is the point where a SEAL is most vulnerable in combat. The boat teams not only take the boats through the surf, they must also haul them up and over some very unforgiving rock piles that jet out into the surf nearby.

A boat crew of BUD/S trainees encounters a wave that may swamp their craft and send them tumbling shoreward. If so, they begin again. As SEALs they will be required to use a rubber raiding boat to come ashore from a submarine or another Special Operations insertion craft, such as the *Mark V* Special Operations Craft (SOC) or a Rigid Hulled Inflatable Boat *(RIB)*. They cannot afford to lose themselves in the surf and their equipment, hence the training. U.S. Navy

Candidates crawl through a forest of concrete pipes with stifling red smoke and explosions to complement their journey. This simulates combat noise and readies the candidate for the future. U.S. Navy

Candidates crouch lower and lower to avoid noise, smoke, and barbed wire. If it was possible to burrow into the earth, they would. This simulates what might happen in a combat situation and is vital for the trainees to understand. Once ashore, often the roughest terrain is the best hiding spot for a SEAL team. U.S. Navy

Because BUD/S training pushes the trainees to the extreme limits of their physical capabilities, safety staff accompany the trainees at all times. They are encouraged to report any illness or defined infirmity that affects a trainee's ability to go on. The Special Warfare training staff does not brutalize the trainees—the course and requirements take all the credit for punishing the would-be SEALs.

Much of the first three weeks of Phase I is spent in determining who has what it takes to continue onward. As noted earlier, this training requires a great resource outlay by the government, and the Navy does not wish to waste a dime. It is important that all of the applicants have a fair opportunity to succeed, but from the Special Warfare standpoint, it is better that the unfit candidates wash out during the training so they end up with qualified people to take their place in the Teams.

This is emphasized so strongly and standards are so high and uncompromising that one entire class failed to complete the course, and none of the applicants graduated to become SEALs.

The fourth week of Phase One training is called "Hell Week," and is designed, in the words of many trainees, to "test the very souls of the candidates." It is not like a hell week in a fraternity or sorority—it is more like hell itself.

Prior to the beginning of Hell Week an instructor will advise the candidates of what is expected and why. They are encouraged to act as a team and not let one another down. They will be asked to participate in a physical exertion program far beyond the reaches of their minds, and do it with virtually no sleep. This week's activities will separate the sheep from the goats, and it is an important step in the evolution of a fully trained SEAL.

BUD/S candidates moving up the beach in a physical training evolution. There is no better method of training than that required at Coronado. U.S. Navy

The slime pit, where candidates must make it across ropes that are continuously being moved about by instructors. Here are three candidates desperately holding on, yet with a sure and certain future of being dunked. U.S. Navy

Another view of the pit where candidates must cross despite harassment from instructors. The mud pits at night during "hell week" also test the mettle of the BUD/S candidates and provide some humor from instructors, who light their way in the darkness. U.S. Navy

Helmets lined in a row abreast of the grinder are mute evidence of those who have left the BUD/S program. Author's Collection

It begins with the usual cold, nighttime shower of seawater punctuated with gunfire and explosives, as well as a confusion of noises, orders, and commands. This is just in the first few minutes, and each candidate knows that there are 120 hours of this and far worse to follow.

The candidates are told to move through one physical training aspect to another, including the obstacle course, small boat operations, and endless calisthenics. They are only allowed four hours of sleep in a specially prepared drafty tent on the beach that is outfitted with canvas cots. The mud pit, which is known to all SEAL applicants that get this far, is a

great source of comedy for those that have gone before. Watching fully grown men sliding and writhing in slimy mud to get them prepared for the worst possible terrain in future missions is funny, but not to those who have mud in every pore and opening in their bodies. Hell week is designed to place the candidate in an extremely stressful environment under the worst of conditions and have them merge as teammates.

Special Warfare staff carefully observe each candidate for signs of illness or physical problems that might be life threatening or lead to injury. Hygiene and medical inspec-

If a candidate wants to voluntarily drop out of the program, this bell must first be rung three times. Then BUD/S is over, and the man can return to his former profession in the Navy. Leaving this training is an agonizing decision, but nonetheless not all are suited for SEAL training. There is surface warfare, aviation, Combat Crew (SWCC), and submarine warfare, and careers are continued without any form of stigma. Author's Collection

A worn and exhausted candidate makes his way across a seaweed-covered beach carrying his weapon. This image conveys much about what a trainee endures during BUD/S and beyond to become a SEAL. U.S. Navy

tions take place every twelve hours, and all candidates eat between 10,000 to 15,000 calories of food per day at four separate meals. They need every calorie of it to survive.

As the candidates that are surviving watch their mental clocks for the magical 120th hour, they notice that up to half of their number have left by voluntarily ringing the ceremonial bell three times and leaving their green helmet, identified with the with class number, on the grinder. There is no shame to ending this ordeal for enlisted man and officer alike. Desire to succeed and sheer courage can carry an individual so far, but man cannot put in what God has left out. Physical strength and endurance must accompany the will to win inside him and among his teammates for success. At the end of the 120 hour period a dirty, sand covered, wet, and shivering man sits with his fellow classmates for a milestone photograph—one that marks a critical step in the successful completion of the U.S. Military's toughest concentrated training.

The completion of Hell week does not mean that all remaining candidates will become SEALs. Quite the contrary is true. Many will leave during the following weeks or in the next phases. Some will leave when they are introduced to water with their hands and feet bound. This evolution is, by its very nature, against the will of an individual to survive. Survival is based on keeping a clear head, and bouncing up and down from the SEAL's swimming pool bottom to capture (or partially capture) a desperately needed breath of air. This often spells doom to the future career of a potential SEAL, but this is the reality of events to come. A SEAL needs to overcome the fear of being trapped and underwater—he must be able to command any situation.

By the time the *Trident* is awarded, only 27% will have been successful in their initial quest to become a SEAL. But the successful completion of Hell week does something to the candidate's attitudes and provides a form of inspiration to

The modern fifty-foot dive tower where BUD/S trainees learn specialized breathing techniques and underwater endurance. Author's Collection

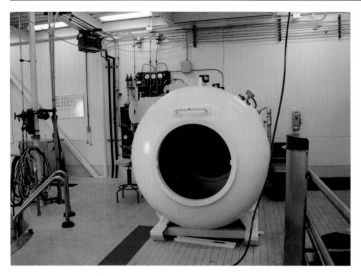

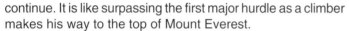

Inside the dive tower at the top, and a miniature dive bell used in training. Author's Collection

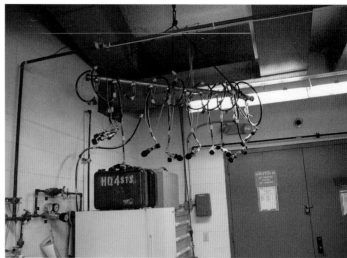

The dive equipment charge/storage room where air tanks are stored and charged for open circuit diving. Author's Collection

continue. It is like surpassing the first major hurdle as a climber makes his way to the top of Mount Everest.

The applicants continue on for another three weeks of intense physical activity, not on the scale of that experienced in Hell week, but equally as grueling and difficult. Most applicants agree that the training is not disappointing—it meets and exceeds their worst nightmares! Despite the frequency of high-risk evolutions (7,500+ annually), Navy Special Warfare has experienced few major injuries and/or deaths due to training. Great care is given by instructors to watch for telltale signs of serious life threatening illness or injury, and those

who are removed from training may be able to rejoin a subsequent class once they have fully recovered.

In Phase II, candidates enter the dive, or waterborne, element of BUD/S training. For many, it will be the first time that they have been exposed to an underwater way of life and diving in general. For some, it will mark the end of BUD/S training, as the drastic change in the type of training often acts as a separator. Men who have been sufficiently able to endure the first eight weeks of physical punishment may not be capable of underwater work. Frankly, this is where the SEALs operate, and up to this point, the training could have

The fifty foot mark of the dive tower shows the opening into which trainees are led down and up by instructors who have demonstrated breathing methods that allow divers to control themselves and their fear underwater. Maintaining self control under water, especially when a severe wave surge tears off your mask and disrupts air supply is essential to the success of a SEAL. Author's Collection

been for any special force. This is where SEALs are distinguished from other Special Forces in the USSOCOM and Marine Corps Reconnaissance forces.

SEALs require extensive and continued physical training that is geared toward a special ability, and that is to operate in water, whether it is inland (rivers, lakes) or the sea. Most of the work that SEALs are assigned involves seaborne assault or reconnaissance, so superior diving skills are an absolute.

The Dive Phase of BUD/s extends for seven weeks and is taught at the Naval Special Warfare Training Center in Coronado, California. Here students are able to use a swimming pool, fifty foot diving tower, and the Pacific Ocean on one side of the base and San Diego Bay on the other.

There are applicants to the program that have never seen an ocean, tasted salt water, or spent any amount of time immersed in water. Some of us tend to forget that most of the United States does not border on the shores of any ocean. This can be a real culture shock to those that have never experienced the sea.

Applicants are trained in the use of several types of underwater breathing systems. The most widely known is the *open circuit system*, which uses an air supply tank and a simple snorkel for short time excursions under the surface. Open circuit air supplies can come from a single or double tank, or from a *SEAL Delivery Vehicle (SDV)* supply system. The *SDV* system is taught later in the training program. The disadvantage of an open circuit system is the tell tale bubbles that emerge on the surface, providing the enemy a "head's up" that divers are below.

A *closed circuit* oxygen underwater breathing apparatus enables the diver to breathe 100% oxygen, so there are no bubbles, and thus no trail for an enemy to detect a SEAL. The *LAR V Draeger* system is used to allow the diver to breathe oxygen, and re-circulates the exhaled breath through a chemical filter that removes carbon dioxide. The unit fits on the chest of the diver and is an excellent means of concealment, but it also has its limitations. There is just so much oxygen that can be stored, and water depth, temperature,

This picture shows a dive suit and accompanying equipment resembling what a SEAL must carry. The Lar V Draeger re-breathing system is shown attached to the front of the model. This system leaves no telltale bubbles and is invaluable for approaching a target without detection. It is a silent method of approaching the enemy, and upgrades to the system will boost endurance from three to four hours. Author's Collection

Dive equipment storage. The Dive phase of BUD/S training first ascertains whether a trainee can stand the rigors of underwater work, and then, if so, the student is taught open and closed circuit diving methods. Author's Collection

and physical exertion affect the capacity of the *Draeger* unit. However, the unit is indispensable to clandestine operations. It will operate for up to four hours under optimum conditions, but under combat conditions, there is no guarantee beyond three hours.

A third option taught is the *closed circuit mixed gas* system underwater breathing apparatus. This system (*Mark 15*) allows the diver to descend to greater depths through the use of a carbon dioxide scrubber canister and the mixture of oxygen and air to maintain an appropriate level of breathable air. The downside of this system can be the need for decompression to prevent the injury or death of the diver.

No system is perfect, and technological advances act as an adjunct to the training a SEAL receives.

Dive training teaches candidates much more than just the use of equipment. It is structured to further build strength and endurance. It also includes exercises to help candidates avoid panic by focusing and thinking through their problems. Without the intellectual power and endurance factors, a diver

The *attack board* or *compass board*, which has been in use for many decades. This simple device in a high tech environment tells time, depth, and direction through the use of a clock, depth gauge, and compass. It is vital to those who travel underwater and at night several feet down. Likely, another tool will come along that does it better, but so far, the *attack board* has been considered a reliable tool for combat divers. Author's Collection

Air tanks for open circuit diving are being charged and stored for use by trainees. Each tank is routinely tested to see that it has adequate pressure. SEAL instructors and trainees alike carefully monitor their equipment for any problems to ensure that everything is thumbs up before a training evolution or mission. Author's Collection

will perish when faced with situations that are temporarily beyond his control. One such form of training makes use of the 50-foot tall dive tower, where candidates are taught specialized breathing techniques to allow them to make a descent and ascent without a stop for air. Trainers watch the candidates carefully to detect any form of panic or frenzy. If a candidate cannot safely endure this type of training then he is unsuitable for future work as a SEAL.

Dive training emphasizes the difficulties that a SEAL will encounter swimming to a target in rough seas or contrary currents. It also reveals those that are not able to endure great stress in an underwater environment. Swimming pools and dive towers are calm, and the beach on the Silver Strand in San Diego is relatively stable, but not all areas in the world are like this. The Persian Gulf reaches temperatures in the hundreds, and work in North Korean waters is near or below freezing. A SEAL has to be able to endure both and complete his mission.

The third and final element of BUD/S training is the Land Warfare Phase, which lasts for ten weeks. It is carried out in deserted areas in the Laguna Mountains near San Diego and the barren and windswept terrain of north San Clemente Island. *Camp Al Huey* is located on San Clemente Island and is exclusive SEAL territory.

As with phase one and two, land warfare reinforces the concept that teamwork without "over the shoulder" supervision is essential once the mission is settled upon. The Laguna Mountains provide an ideal area for training SEAL applicants in land navigation and fieldwork, including negotiating difficult terrain without leaving signs. They dress, eat, and live like their predecessors from World War II, Korea, Vietnam, and the Persian Gulf. It is here that a SEAL trainee begins to resemble a real SEAL.

By the time the remaining members of any particular class are moved to San Clemente Island, the class can be down to 10% of its original number. It is at this point that a class may be increased in number by those that have trained to that point but were injured and have mended sufficiently to continue onward. They are called "roll backs," and they become members of the current class. If a candidate is injured in an earlier phase in the training they may also join a new class where they left off, providing that they did not voluntarily give up and their injury has healed sufficiently.

In Camp Al Huey, reconnaissance, live fire exercises, Immediate Action Drills (IAD), weapons usage, small unit tactics, and combat demolition of explosives are ground into the applicants. Training never seems to cease as the SEAL candidates learn their trade on the ground. Many applicants have never fired an automatic weapon before, and rarely have any fired a fully automatic M-60 machine gun. Here they do this and more, including a number of highly realistic live fire exercises. Applicants are trained and retrained in night swimming. Some instructors feel that it is beneficial to show shark films and movies to the swimmers before they enter the Santa Barbara Channel for a multi-mile combat swim. There are manta rays and sharks in the area, so cautionary words are spoken—*watch out for yourselves and your team members*.

Demolition of obstacles in the water is also taught in this phase. This practice dates back to the early 1940s when UDT swimmers attached charges to enemy placed concrete and steel impediments, as well as coral heads. Invasion beaches must be cleared before troops can land, and six decades after it began it continues today. Training in land warfare is performed in daylight to enable instructors to observe the trainees, but all SEAL operations rely on darkness as an ally. Training at night will be in a future segment of the program.

One Day and its All Over – Graduation

For all, the day BUD/S comes to an end is a major accomplishment in their military and personal lives. BUD/S reveals weaknesses, yet it also brings out strengths in character and leadership that a candidate may not have been aware of. The Navy formally honors those who made it at the same place where they began—on the grinder. One graduation speaker put it in terms that all can understand, "a world that

A three man patrol has taken up position to defend its area during the Laguna Mountains phase of land warfare. The stint in the Laguna Mountains gives the BUD/S trainee the feel for land warfare, weapons, map reading, and working as a team while ashore. The man to the extreme right has a grenade launcher as part of his weapons package. U.S. Navy

rewards mediocrity is fascinated by an individual or individuals that have achieved the impossible." For the 27% and sometimes lower number of a particular class, the almost impossible has been achieved. Recently, a class of 150 only graduated 25, and the Navy needs 40 per class to maintain a credible force of SEALs. But there is no offer to compromise the high standards of SEAL training—and it is not likely that this offer will ever come.

The end of BUD/S training does not entitle a graduate to wear the coveted *Trident (U.S. Navy Special Warfare Pin)*. Next comes Jump School at Fort Benning, Georgia, to enable each candidate to develop his airborne competency. He has already achieved success on the ground and in the water, but the third element that enables a candidate to become a SEAL is being able to insert into a target area from the air. Prospective SEALs are taught the proper way to use a combat parachute and how to insert within a few feet of a designated target area. Simply teaching an applicant to safely land on the ground is not sufficient for the skills required on SEAL missions. He must feel comfortable in the air, be able to exit a high-speed aircraft at great altitudes, and land where he supposed to. Once this is learned it is continually reinforced in future training.

Prospective SEALs learn static line jumping with a MCI-IB parachute for low altitude jumping (800 feet), and the MT1XS system for free falls from (e.g. 25,000-2,500 feet) altitude. The MT1XS is termed as a ram-air canopy and can be highly maneuverable in the hands of a proficient jumper. Air dropping of cargo, including rubber raiding craft, is also learned.

After the successful completion of jump training the candidate enters the third element of SEAL training. This was once known as SEAL Tactical Training (STT); however, the name has been changed to SEAL Qualification Training (SQT), and like other programs is taught in Coronado, California, at the Naval Special Warfare Training Center. It is a fifteen-week course that covers a myriad of subjects necessary to round out the candidate's skills, and at the same time identifies areas where a particular candidate has superior ability.

The course outline includes the following:
- **Medical training** to enable treatment of severe trauma and battle wounds that are most common. Dive related disorders also occupy a place in this training.
- **Communications training**, including the use and repair of high tech radios and communications equipment.

Congratulations to those who have completed an element of the training. The red line holds the cap of the trainee to prevent head covers from floating out to sea during surf operations and other evolutions. U.S. Navy

Class 232 celebrates graduation from BUD/ S. This formal ceremony signifies that the surviving candidates of the most rigorous military training in the world have made it. Included in this class are a Korean naval officer and a chief petty officer from the same navy. Two other graduates were a naval officer from Thailand and one from Peru. U.S. Navy Special Warfare training is considered the best worldwide, and the more foreign naval trainees that graduate, the better for networking in times of crisis. Courtesy, U.S. Navy Special Warfare Center.

- **Land Navigation training** to enable SEAL teams to pinpoint locations and target areas for night landings in hostile and unfamiliar territory.
- **Weapons training**, including use and repair, as well as developing keen marksmanship.
- **Urban assault training,** which includes dealing with friendly or hostile civilian encounters while on a mission and knowing how and when to react.
- **Combat swimming training** includes learning to swim in a combat environment while carrying a heavy load of weapons and other gear.
- **Tactical weapons and demolitions training** teach the knowledgeable and proper use of explosives, which is clearly an important tool for a SEAL.
- **Air Operations training**, including helicopter insertion and extraction training.

These training classes are not merely a refresher course for what has already been learned, but further reinforce earlier exposure to all of the skills required of a SEAL. Success in this training program comes from a near superhuman degree of personal commitment and desire to become a SEAL.

At the end of the Seal Qualification Training course the Trident is awarded, and after a year of training the SEAL can be assigned to a team. However, he is on probation, which lasts six months. At the end of this time, the new SEAL can rest, but just for a few minutes. What came before in training will continue in reality throughout a SEAL's career. The only thing that is different from training is that combat or a critical mission is but a telephone call away. Trainees do not fight and risk their lives—SEALs do.

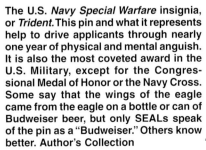

The U.S. *Navy Special Warfare* insignia, or *Trident.* This pin and what it represents help to drive applicants through nearly one year of physical and mental anguish. It is also the most coveted award in the U.S. Military, except for the Congressional Medal of Honor or the Navy Cross. Some say that the wings of the eagle came from the eagle on a bottle or can of Budweiser beer, but only SEALs speak of the pin as a "Budweiser." Others know better. Author's Collection

Chapter 4

Equipment and Weapons Systems

When combat is imminent, it is the training, teamwork, and know how that count. But it is also important that the Seals be outfitted with proven equipment and weapons. Each SEAL mission is planned very carefully to ensure operational success. Considerable thought is given to the number of personnel that will be used and selection of equipment and weapons. A specific target may only require an eight man squad delivered by a RIB boat and a Combat Rubber Raiding Craft (CRRC) to a hostile beach. However, in another instance a full platoon of sixteen men might be dropped by parachute. Generally, a platoon is the maximum number of SEALs required for most missions.

To a large degree the government provides the equipment used by the SEALs, but there are items that individual SEALs often purchase for themselves to augment navy issue.

SEALs camouflage their equipment bases upon the terrain of their prospective mission. This usually involves painting and using duct tape to ensure that their weapons, ammunition, and any other pieces of equipment do not stand out. What good does it do to paint your face to blend in with the jungle or desert, yet have shiny brass cartridges in an ammunition bandoleer around your arm as shown in some of the

movies about special warfare? Uniforms (BDUs), helmets, and netting used to cover them must also conform to the intended terrain. Equipment painted to match a particular camouflage pattern (e.g. Desert or Jungle, etc.) is termed "boflage." "Over the counter" dive masks, flexible fins, and knives are among those items that are frequently purchased by SEALs, however, with the popularity of masks in iridescent pink and purple colors, the old standby dull black is getting more difficult to find. "Local dive shop" equipment usually needs to be fully camouflaged before it can become part of a SEAL's outfit.

A key piece of equipment that is carried by men in a SEAL Team is mission specific communication systems, which can range from hand-held radios to satellite link-ups that allow long distance transmissions. There are those among the SEALs that prefer sophisticated communications, which permit higher authority to be in constant contact, but that is a matter of operational protocol. Aside from the more exotic items carried by Naval Special Warfare personnel, there are other items just as necessary. A dependable watch, maps, and money are old standbys, as well as cordage and a small signal mirror. First aid kits for wound treatment, a compass, and chemical lights are also part of the kit. Clean water is a

A Combat Rubber Raiding Craft (CRRC) powered by an outboard motor (likely a 35 hp Johnson or Evinrude), which has been painted to match the boat. The CRRC can be inflated in 45 seconds, and carries a SEAL squad that is heavily armed with a variety of weapons selected for a particular mission. The CRRC is generally used for insertion and extraction of SEAL personnel into hostile territory. U.S. Navy

must, as well as food. The food ration generally comes in the form of Meals, Ready to Eat (MRE), which has a shelf life of three years and comes in 24 selections. MREs are nutritious, and when supplemented by high-energy bars can provide a SEAL with sufficient energy. It should be noted, however, that no one has yet opened a MRE fashionable restaurant in any major city. As a result, SEALs frequently supplement rations with snack items found at local Wal-Marts and other stores. SEAL operators are careful not leave evidence of their passing, so scented colognes, shaving lotions, and other telltale items are forbidden. An enemy can even smell the difference between an American made cigarette and those locally produced. Dependent on the mission, handcuffs, anti-personnel mines, and camouflage netting may be included, however, the more items, the more difficult for a man to operate. Of greatest importance is the weapons suite selected.

Weapons Used by Naval Special Warfare - SEALs

Heavy firepower available on the patrol boats (PC), Mark Vs, and even the 11 meter Rigid Hulled Inflatable Boats (RIB) consists of .50 caliber dual and single barrel machines guns, 25 millimeter guns, 40mm grenade launchers, M-60 machine guns, and short range "Stinger" handheld missiles. Not much of a comparison to laser guided munitions (big deck carrier aircraft), Harpoon and Tomahawk missiles (Los Angeles and Virginia class submarines and Aegis class destroyers and cruisers), and five-inch/54 or 62 cal guns aboard cruisers and destroyers. On the other hand, cruisers, destroyers, aircraft carriers, and submarines cannot cruise close to the surf-line of a hostile beach—SEALs and the Combat Crew do. The armament on the boats is used as a protective shield for the SEALs as they come and go on their nightly missions.

SOG Bowie S1

SOG Seal-Knife 2000

SOG Seal Pup

A single .50 caliber machine (foreground) and a double barrel .50 caliber machine gun in the background aboard a *Mark V* Special Operations Craft *(SOC)* in Coronado, California, January 2001. The single .50 caliber machine gun has yet to be provided with ammunition, however, its twin version is loaded for bear. These types of weapons and others aboard the offshore craft are designed to protect the boats and the SEALs as they come and go. Author's Collection

A selection of commercial knives offered by the SOG Company. The original SOG Bowie S1 was replicated after the Vietnam War era Studies and Observation Group (SOG) knife that was developed. The SOG Seal Knife 2000 and SEAL Pup Knife are sold to the SEAL teams in large numbers and are well thought of. The SOG Bowie S1 retails for nearly $300 and is considered a classic knife. Courtesy SOG Knives

SEALs employ a number of low and high tech weapons that *must* function at all times, and they go to great lengths to protect them from the elements. SEALs rarely spray bullets at a target, and prefer to use as little ammunition as possible to achieve their goals. Due to weight constraints SEALs carry only those items needed for the job at hand, and dependent on the mission they carry a variety of weapons. A fire team (four men), squad (eight men), or platoon (sixteen SEALs) generally vary their weapons and equipment packages, just as they diversify their primary skills. The most commonly used weapons are:

A well dressed Special Warfare combatant complete with goggles, vest, and a rubberized version of the Heckler and Kock MP-5 submachine gun. This mannequin is located in the armory of SEAL Team Three based in Coronado, California. Author's Collection

- Specialized knives made by SOG. The SEALs often ask for the SEAL "pup," which is a small knife, and the larger SEAL knife 2000, which is the official knife approved by Naval Special Warfare. This knife has a seven-inch stainless steel blade with a coated black surface. The 5.25 inch handle is made from glass reinforced Zytel, and the sheath is made of black cordura. To secure official approval from Naval Special Warfare this knife had to pass a series of tests that would demolish an ordinary knife, but most knives do not endure the punishment a SEAL can deliver. The design of these knives is based upon the famous Bowie knife of the early 1800s. There are those who prefer other knives, including bayonets that have been machine honed to meet the personal taste of the SEAL. Many carry simple pocket knives for everyday use and not for stealth operations. In any event, a knife is intensely personal to a SEAL.

- Nine millimeter SIG Sauer P-226 handgun (fifteen rounds), which is a semiautomatic weapon capable of a 50-meter effective range.

- Smith and Wesson six shot .357-caliber revolver. The model 686, which weighs 41 ounces, is a popular but dated weapon without sophisticated electronics and laser sighting. *However, when all else fails, it won't.* Sand, water, dirt, and jungle humidity do not affect this weapon, hence its value.

- Mark 23 Special Application handgun (45 caliber). This weapon weighs 2.42 pounds and has a fifty-meter effective range.

- Heckler and Kock MP-5SD (9 millimeter) submachine gun with built in noise suppressor. It has a stated effective range of 100 meters, but it is most useful at less than 25-30 meters.

- Heckler and Kock MP-5 (9 millimeter) submachine gun without noise suppressor.

- Mark 14 (updated M–60 machine gun). This is the bread and butter weapon for laying down a field of fire. It weighs 20.8 pounds and is typically operated by one SEAL.

- M-4/A-1 Carbine. The new Special Operations Peculiar Modification (SOPMOD) Accessory Kit has recently been approved for use by Special Forces. It includes a carrying handle that doubles as a sight; M-203 grenade launchers with QD mount; nine volt visible light; AN/PEQ-2 infrared pointer/illuminator for ranges up to 600 meters; rail interface system; QD sound suppressor (30 decibel re-

A rogue's gallery of weapons displayed at the U.S. Navy Special Warfare Center in Coronado, California (SEAL Team Three). Each SEAL team has its own armory and series of dedicated buildings and storage facilities. Permission to enter is difficult to negotiate, even for other SEAL teams. This is considered private property and is well cared for by well-trained and schooled staff. The engraved plastic cards in front of each weapon are not there for tourists or even writers—they are used for trainee orientation to various weapons they may use in combat. Staff maintains a strict inventory of all equipment at all times. Author's Collection

The SIG Suaer P226 handgun, which is a favorite among SEALs. It is semiautomatic and effective up to 50 meters. It fires a 9 mm round, and is primarily used in close quarters. Author's Collection

A six shot Magnum .357 handgun. Despite its commonality and the fact that the weapon represents ancient technology, it works when it is supposed to work. This is its strongest recommendation and makes it very popular. Author's Collection

duction); and Advanced Combat Optical Gun Sight (ACOG), 4X sight, and reflex sight out to 600 meters. The M-4/A-1 fires a 5.56mm round.

- M-79 Grenade Launcher, which was originally designed six decades ago. The M-79 fires all types of grenades (fragmentation, smoke, stun, etc.).
- M-14 Sniper Rifle. This is an automatic loading 7.62-millimeter caliber sniper rifle capable of accuracy out to 800 meters.
- McBrous M-88 .50 caliber special application sniper rifle. These weapons weigh 27.18 pounds and up to four are carried per platoon. This weapon is probably the most destructive of all long range sniper rifles in the world.

Aside from handguns, grenade launchers, machine guns, and sniper rifles, SEALs employ 12 gauge Mossberg shot-

guns, mortars, rocket launchers, grenades, and other munitions. The Chinese Communist (Chicom) type 56 or AK-47 of foreign manufacture is also used. SEALs spend time familiarizing themselves with other nation's weaponry. This can mean the difference between life and death. Being able to secure your enemy's weapon and use it is a vital element of close-range combat.

Being able to see if your enemy is present and his number at night or in murky weather is one of the major assets contributing to success in Naval Special Warfare. Although it is common to watch SEALs exercise and practice in the daylight, this is done to allow instructors and leaders to observe the men at work. Virtually all SEAL missions take place in darkness, for the night is an ally. Piercing through the dark often means the use of infrared sighting and thermal imaging. Also used are *AN/PV* (single eye) night vision devices

A Mark 23 .45 caliber special application handgun. It weighs nearly 2 1/2 pounds, but packs quite a punch. It is almost like a side arm cannon, yet has a noise suppressor and can be fitted with a laser-aiming module. Author's Collection

Petty Officer Pence holds a German manufactured Heckler & Kock MP-55SD, which has a built in stainless steel noise suppressor. The weapon does not require sub-sonic ammunition. Its range is 100 meters and weighs 7.14 pounds. Author's Collection

A Heckler & Kock MP-5 without noise suppressor. It has a 30 round magazine and has a sling for its operator to carry it close to firing position at all times. Special Warfare is generally fought in close quarters, and weapons of this type are invaluable. Author's Collection

A Mark 23 Model 0 machine gun that fires a 7.62mm round. This 20.8-pound weapon is considered lightweight, and can lay down a field of fire that is almost guaranteed to destroy an onrushing enemy, or at least keep their heads down until the SEALs have left the area. Author's Collection

that can be submerged up to 30 meters and still be serviceable. Ironically, *Leggs* pantyhose are purchased (color coordinated) to prevent sand and dirt from getting into the optics.

Explosives

There are other weapons and systems used by the SEALs. Often, the task is *to get in, set explosive charges, and leave undetected*. This charge can be on the hull of a ship with a World War II era designed "limpet mine." The limpet mine is simply an explosive charge that is carried underwater to a

target hull and attached to the hull via magnets. A timer is set, and when contact is made, a hole is blown in the hull of a vessel. A timer will set off the charge after the SEALs have left the area. The hole may not sink the ship, but its placement is certain to immobilize it for a long period of time.

A satchel charge, which is a bag filled with explosives, can be used to blow up beach obstacles. This is particularly effective against hardened targets (concrete) and prior to an amphibious landing. Satchel charges can be used against targets ashore and have been since the mid 1940s in the

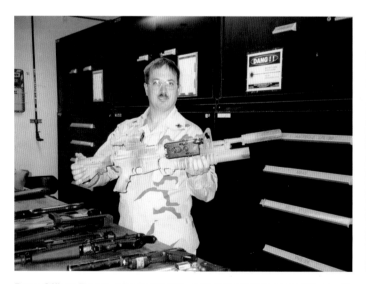

Petty Officer Pence, who is wearing a desert warfare camouflage uniform including insignia, holds one of the most powerful submachine guns available. This is the multi-functional M4/A-1. It is known as the "junkyard dog without a bark." It can be fitted with a noise suppressor, "ACOG" (Advanced Combat Optical Gunsight), and grenade launcher. For some SEALs it is too complex, yet it is accurate to 500 meters and for most considered to be the workhorse of Naval Special operations. Its rail system allows other weapon enhancements to be added dependent on mission need. Author's Collection

The M-79 grenade launcher is carried by a member of a team to lay down short-range explosives, such as fragmentation, smoke for escape and evasion, and stun variants. It dates back to World War II, yet like so many tried and true weapons, if it works—use it. Author's Collection

The M14 Sniper Rifle, which fires a 7.62mm round. This weapon provides a sniper team (shooter and spotter) with a weapon that is effective up to 800 meters. Sniper training is conducted at the Army equivalent of Naval Special Warfare at Fort Bragg, North Carolina. A sniper is unique in warfare. He fights alone, and if not cautious, dies the same way. By their very nature snipers are careful and observant. They may wait for a target for days, and that means they are also disconcertingly patient—this alone makes them highly dangerous. Snipers must shoot in the highest category to earn their rating. Author's Collection

The big bad boy of sniper rifles is the McBrous M-88, .50-caliber bolt-action weapon with a 2,000-meter range. It is powerful enough to crack an iron engine block and disable trucks and other vehicles at great distances. It is also sufficient to guarantee results when used against human target(s). Up to four of these weapons are assigned to a SEAL platoon. Author's Collection

Pacific. It is estimated that the limpet mine and satchel charge will continue to be among the explosives of choice in Naval Special Warfare for many years.

Dynamite and plastic explosives are also used, such as C-4. C-4 is a plastic type of explosive that is highly stable and pliable, and resembles plumber's putty. It can be placed in any number of locations and in any number of shapes. Explosives are detonated by fuse or electrically, but in any event, SEAL operators prefer to be far away.

Dynamite is not held in as great esteem as it once was. At one time it was popular as a mass detonator for gasoline and other chemical drums located in target areas. Today, "mission specific" munitions and explosives have generally replaced localized improvisation. More extensive pre-planning plays a greater part in all special warfare operations.

A lightweight thermal imaging sight. Being that this type of equipment will be transported through water, waterproofing is difficult. Sand and other debris is kept out of optical instruments with pantyhose. Often the least expensive and at the same time obvious means make things happen for Naval Special Warfare. Author's Collection

AN/PVS-18 eyepiece for night vision. This device will withstand depths of 30 meters, and is considered one of the better eyepieces at $10,000. It is rarely loaned out to other units. Author's Collection

A live fire exercise being held by a SEAL team while on duty in Bosnia in July 1997. The exercise is being held in a deserted sandpit. U.S. Navy

A satchel charge that is used by SEALs to destroy beach obstacles and other hardened targets. This particular charge was photographed at the Naval Special Warfare Center in January 2001. UDT Frogmen during the latter part of World War II could also be seen using similar explosives on coral heads and other island defense laid down by the Japanese prior to an invasion by Allied forces. Author's Collection

Communications

SEALs must be able to communicate with insertion and extraction forces and amongst themselves. This begins with simple hand signals. A halt sign means just that—*stop at once.* Two fingers pointed at his eyes by the leader means "enemy in sight," and a lowering of the hand means "take cover." Aside from darkness, silence is also an ally to the SEALs.

Moving up the technological chain of communications, the men on the ground use a line of sight handset with earphones and microphone, but hills and other major obstructions do interfere. All of the team members have radios, and generally, for a large-scale operation three or more spare units

are carried. There are also VHF and UHF radios for outside communications. The UHF set will transmit from ground to air to a range of 50 miles antenna to antenna. The high frequency set will transmit and receive over hundreds of miles.

One new system, the PSE-5 UHF/VHF, costs upwards of $25,000 and employs a laptop personal computer that is connected to a satellite antenna. Lithium batteries are used that keep a charge for an extended period, but unfortunately cannot be recharged. Another option are the Nicad batteries that can be recharged, but add too much weight to an often already overburdened SEAL. What is used depends on the mission. One thing is always present, and that is a SEAL with

An example of a portable radio used by the SEALs to maintain contact. When a radio fails, it is up to a communications specialist to find the trouble and fix it. They are often considered magicians when they bring a muddy water logged unit back to life. Author's Collection

A complex setup for long-range communications that includes a laptop computer. This represents a cost of $25,000 to the taxpayers, and is worth every penny when it is being used by men far away from friendly forces. This is the PSE-5 UHF/VHF satellite system. The laptop was turned off when we entered the communications shack to photograph the unit. Author's Collection

The "pelican case," which is used to carry sensitive communication equipment and hopefully keep it dry. It is attached to the back of the communicator and is closed like a "zip-lock" bag to seal out moisture. Author's Collection

A member of SEAL Team offsite based at Coronado, California, employs a Nikon/Kodak DCS 425 underwater digital camera to relay *real time* images to leadership. To supplement the images, an LPI LPD tracking device converts mission status and longitude/latitude to brevity codes and sends them to decision makers. This makes the situation "up close and personal" for those waiting at situation and planning sites. U.S. Navy

exceptional electronic ability. When radio equipment is dragged through the mud, water, sand, and dirt, it is certain to fail unless an expert (magician) can make it work. Each team has just such a magician. Of course, the sand, dirt, water, and mud is somewhat deterred by "pelican cases," which are "ruggedized" waterproof zip-lock carriers.

In addition to inter/intra Team communication, there is also the need to transmit information to ships and amphibious units before they mount an invasion, open fire with five inch mounts, or launch Tomahawk missiles at selected targets. SEALs provide reconnaissance and observation services that prevent the needless waste of expensive munitions and men. For this, they may use something as elementary as a hand mirror or a basic signal light for night communications. Despite the onset of more and more sophisticated (and expensive) equipment, it is often the simple methods that work best.

Technology has also provided the SEALs with the global positioning system (GPS). A GPS can tell a team or an individual member where they are within a few feet on the earth. While maps, compasses, and information on the area of operations are still important, a GPS receiver has become integral to field operations. Ironically, this type of technology has become so common that many auto manufacturers utilize a GPS to locate drivers that have become lost. So, in the early 21st century the GPS is already almost commonplace. However, the technology does point toward some rather exciting possibilities for the future of SEAL team operations

In the hand of SEALs, specialized weapons, explosives, and communications equipment make them a potent force. When they are not on a mission, SEALs are training. Their equipment is likewise kept in the best condition possible and stored in lockers that are protected from outsiders—including members from other SEAL teams. This way, everything is kept on the up and up.

During an amphibious exercise entitled "Kernel Blitz" in 1995, SEALs signal an LCAC (landing craft air cushion) with the information necessary to make a safe landing. Being on the beach first to remove obvious danger and provide reconnaissance is something the SEALs do best, and it is appreciated by the Navy and Marine Corps when they come ashore to take an objective. U.S. Navy

Chapter 5

SEAL Team Operations - Insertion/Extraction Platforms

Getting everyone back at the end of a mission is an absolute among the SEALs. They do not leave one of their own behind. That is part of their credo, code, and doctrine. Integral to this code are the methods by which they arrive in hostile territory and then how they exit. There is not always a friendly helicopter pilot with his rotors turning or a Combat Crewmember in a RIB with its engines gurgling awaiting a squad of exhausted men. Sometimes, a SEAL squad and its members are required to take evasive maneuvers and escape paths to exit enemy controlled areas. Whether extraction is simple or difficult, SEALs do not leave a wounded team member behind. The special boat crews, helicopter pilots, and others who work closely with this community of men respect this doctrine. They do their best to accommodate the SEALs no matter what the venue—air, surface, or subsurface. However, even though a mission does not begin with an exit, it is an important consideration in the mission planning process.

Missions and Operations

Unlike most films, many magazine articles, and unfortunately "tell-all" books, operations do not originate overnight, nor are they carried out by trainees or those with little experience. SEAL teams have areas of responsibility that span the globe. In a very real sense, the world is their battlefield. A mission may involve an operation that needs immediate attention, or one that has been brewing for a long period of time. In many cases, the Naval Special Warfare Center has already brainstormed contingencies for most of the possible operations and are a step ahead in planning when an assignment comes down. Seeking out, capturing, or killing the ringleaders of the terrorist cells that planned, supported, and/or financed the September 11, 2001, attacks on the World Trade Center and the Pentagon may be a roll assigned to a SEAL team. Special Operations now appears to be the ideal solution in the early 21st century for prosecuting a war that is unconventional and face to face with the sworn enemies of the United States and other freedom loving nations.

A SEAL carefully watches a beach area prior to a landing by a Landing Craft Air Cushion, or *"LCAC,"* as it is known. He has just checked the coordinates of the landing zone for the *LCAC* and will signal that it is safe to invade soon. U.S. Navy

Right: An *LCAC* filled with vital supplies, equipment, and Marines requires a beach to land on that is unobstructed and devoid of heavy enemy resistance. SEAL operatives research and reconnoiter a landing site to ensure a successful invasion by these 40+ knot capable vessels. The range of the air cushioned, 194 ton fully loaded *LCAC* is 200 nautical miles, and can be launched over the horizon for a surprise attack—providing the SEALs have paved the way. Its air cushion allows the *LCAC* to push upward to dry land and not be stopped at the surf line. U.S. Navy

Below, Right: The Echo platoon of SEAL Team Two has just boarded (via fast roping) the Aegis class cruiser *USS Normandy CG-60* in the Red Sea on a search and *take down* exercise. Elements of SEAL Team Two are assigned to the carrier battle group spearheaded by the *USS George Washington CVN-73*. This exercise took place on July 21, 2000. U.S. Navy

The origin of missions comes from higher authority, and that means a theater commander or the Pentagon. SEAL teams do not originate their own missions, except when they have been assigned to an operation with a lengthy duration. An example of this was in Vietnam, where SEAL teams were assigned to various geographical areas to interdict enemy supply routes or destroy enemy strongpoints. Even in this environment, orders came down to operate in a specific locale and then generally disrupt enemy operations, including specific targets.

When an operation has been decided upon, it is up to U.S. Special Operations Command (USSOCOM) to determine what forces are necessary to bring a mission to a successful conclusion. The requesting authority (Joint Chiefs of Staff, Theater Commander, etc.) is kept in the communications loop, but with a lower degree of continuous operational

The Aegis class cruiser *USS Normandy CG-60* comes alongside the *Nimitz* class nuclear carrier *USS George Washington CVN-73*. Both vessels are part of a larger battlegroup and include a SEAL Team as part of its force composition. U.S. Navy

What the business end of a SEAL looks like as he waits for an order to fire his weapon or move to another vantage point. SEAL team members support one another in a prearranged fashion that is continuously planned and prepared for. U.S. Navy

What a well-dressed SEAL sniper wears (togs) in combat or during training. A sniper can wait hours or days for an opportunity to carry out his mission. It is a lonely profession and requires a high degree of patience. This was part of an annual demonstration at the UDT-SEAL Museum at Fort Pierce, Florida. The SEALs are a tight knit group with their UDT/Frogmen forefathers and always enjoy a visit to the museum that honors them. Courtesy UDT/SEAL Museum

detail. With the sophisticated communications equipment now available, it is possible for the President of the United States to speak directly to a hidden SEAL sniper in Central America, but this scenario is absurd!

If the SEALs and/or Combat Crew are involved, the fine points of what is needed are transmitted to the Commander, Naval Special Warfare to design and bring to fruition a plan. This may include other elements of Army or Air Force Special Operations, and often includes the use of "big Navy" assets, such as naval aircraft. SEAL teams need to be able to rely upon air support and naval gunfire, if necessary, so preparations include this and respective local commanders are alerted. Planning begins with deciding how the objective can be achieved, and then the process moves to how the inser-

tion will be made and then the exit or extraction. Assets for the mission down to the last piece of equipment are decided upon, as well as collateral organizations that need to participate.

The SEALs have no dedicated rotary wing (helicopters) or fixed wing aircraft, and must rely on the navy or other service branch air assets. For high altitude parachute drops, Air Force Special Operations is called upon to become part of a plan.

Most of the operations that require the SEALs and/or Combat Crew and their craft are small, yet vital. They do not include the employment of large numbers of men, although there are those in military leadership that see the SEALs fighting in regimental or company size strength. The idea of sev-

SEALs exit a CH-53E "Sea Stallion" helicopter during an exercise in Bosnia in July 1997. In this evolution, the helo lights quickly, the SEALs exit, and the Helo is then history. U.S. Navy

SEAL operatives demonstrate technique and equipment for visitors at the UDT-SEAL Museum in Fort Pierce, Florida. These men have just been fast roped to their landing zone and are performing a simulated approach to a target for the audience, which includes several high level Special Forces personnel. SEALs rarely show themselves off in public. Courtesy UDT/SEAL Museum

Old "Victory" type ships at the Suisun Bay Reserve Fleet in Suisun Bay, California. These vessels are often used in "ship take down" exercises by the SEALs. Unfortunately, one exercise led to an explosive charge blowing a hole in the side of the selected vessel that almost caused it to sink. Author's Collection

A U.S. Navy "Seahawk" helicopter hovers in the background after lowering SEALs to a landing zone. This rotary wing aircraft was used in a mock exercise at the UDT/SEAL Museum in Fort Pierce, Florida. Courtesy UDT/SEAL Museum

eral hundred well trained men committed to a battle is appealing to those who do not understand that the operational strong suit of naval special operations lies in small unit combat and stealth.

In the late 20th century and certainly in the early 21st century, the SEALs have been and will be called up for the following missions—all of which involve getting their feet wet. These operations are more commonly expected, but there is no limitation as to what might be asked. They are preceded by a "Warning Order," which notifies personnel of an impending operation. This is a formalized statement that by its very existence conveys the critical nature of what is being ordered.

• Hydrographic reconnaissance of prospective beachheads for Marine Expeditionary Unit invasions. This involves a thorough examination of an area, including the surrounding waters, and making notes on something as simple as a slate with a grease pencil. Natural and man-made obstacles, including fortifications, need to be plotted, and then invasion leaders briefed on what to expect. This can also include reconnaissance of beachheads that may deceive the enemy as to the intentions of our armed forces. Disinformation can be a powerful tool in warfare.

• Hydrographic research and then destruction of manmade or natural barriers to an invasion on an intended beachhead. This means setting charges and detonating them as a prelude to an invasion or a feinted invasion. Again, disinformation can be a powerful weapon and cause enemy forces to divert valuable forces and reinforcements needlessly.

• Ship, aircraft, or structure *takedowns*. This entails boarding a ship or hostile grounded aircraft, which may have hostages aboard, and saving them while capturing or killing their captors. In the age of terrorism, kidnapping, and hijacking (near east, central America, east Africa, Balkans, and now

A member of SEAL Team Eight covers his squad from the doorway of a *SH-60 "Seahawk"* helicopter. They have just begun a board, search, and seizure mission on the 6th Fleet Command ship, the *USS La Salle AGF-3*, in this May 20, 1996, image. Seahawk helicopter variants have been armed with six barrel 7.62 mm mini-guns and the more common 7.62mm machine gun. This type of firepower plus rockets provides SEAL operators with accurate and deadly covering fire, if needed. U.S. Navy

the U.S.), the SEALs are an ideal force for countering this type of activity. Saving hostages and at the same time sending a notice to would-be terrorists that a SEAL team visit will be imminent provides a great deterrent.

- Capturing a prisoner or prisoners to gain intelligence for a mission. This kind of operation involves coming ashore at night, removing individuals, and gathering information without a trace. It is one of the more exotic yet viable tasks that SEALs can perform.
- Taking captured American or allied prisoners from their captors through direct action.

- Harbor sabotage by setting explosive charges at strategic points and under the hulls of hostile vessels or vessels containing contraband.
- Working with allied nations in various operations that involve waterborne attack. This includes foreign internal defense (FID) aid, advice, and assistance in various aspects of unconventional warfare.
- Unconventional warfare by working with allied guerilla forces through training and equipping partisans and those sympathetic to American and allied interests.

SEALs may leave their home ground without all of the equipment necessary for a mission. This is true when additional intelligence surfaces that requires other pieces of hardware. For this contingency, the Air Deployable Delivery System (ADDS) has been developed. Two aviation mates are about to drop an ADDS to a waiting SEAL Team from the *USS Tempest PC-2*, a coastal patrol gunboat. This photograph was taken in August 1997 near the coast of Italy. U.S. Navy

The nuclear attack submarine *USS Greeneville SSN-772* in late January 2001. The *SEAL Delivery Vehicle (SDV)* capable *Los Angeles* class submarine was making a port visit to the San Francisco Bay and shortly thereafter returned to Pearl Harbor. Author's Collection

Sponsons on the deck aft of the sail used to carry a dry-deck shelter (DDS), or the new Advanced Seal Delivery System (ASDS) being tested in Pearl Harbor. There are fifteen ASDS mini submarines planned for the future, dependent on the outcome of the test vehicle. The *USS Greeneville SSN-772* has been used for these tests. Author's Collection

An Ohio class ballistic missile submarine. This type of submersible is slated to carry an ASDS, as are selected Los Angeles class attack submarines. The modified Ohio class will be able to carry two ASDS as opposed to one on the attack boats. Four of the Ohio class are to be fitted to carry land and maritime attack guided missiles similar to Russian Oscar class guided missile submarines. U.S. Navy

- Counter terrorism, which includes the destruction of terrorists and their strongholds and equipment storage sites. Counter terrorism can also take the form of training locals in terrorism suppression and deterrence. Seeking out terrorists to bring them to justice or destroy those who resist.

SEAL team members have direct input into the details of an operation, and in the face of requests that seem to be doomed to fail, they do object in the strongest terms. Sending a SEAL squad to assault a heavily defended enemy stronghold may exceed their realistic capability and waste resources. Foolhardy suggestions by military theorists are not tolerated.

The Trip in and Out

After the details of an operation or training mission have been settled upon, transportation to and from the objective is determined. A part of the decision making process involves what assets are immediately available or can be diverted by another command. This and other logistical questions have to be answered during the planning stages, including a series of contingencies. One of the least desirable contingencies is through escape and evasion, thus making the best of a bad situation. In any event, there are two major requirements. They are stealth going in and exit successfully with retrieval of all the team members.

This can be achieved by a number of transportation means, including s*ea*, *air*, and/or *land.* The primary insertion and extraction means are as follows.

An artist's rendering of the Advanced Seal Delivery System (ASDS) being tested at Pearl Harbor. The ASDS has a passenger/cargo space that is dry lockout for exit/entry and control station. The ASDS is being built by Northrop-Grumman Ocean Systems, displaces 55 tons, and is 65 feet long. It is powered by a 67hp electric motor with a top speed of eight knots for a range up to 125 nautical miles. It will be crewed by an officer and an enlisted man and will carry a SEAL squad of eight men. U.S. Navy

The ASDS prototype being tested on the east coast in ice cold waters. The tests have been quite successful. Northrop-Grumman.

A dry-deck shelter *(DDS)* aboard one of the older converted ballistic missile submarines. The converted ballistic missile boats can carry two DDS, which in turn can carry a Seal Delivery Vehicle *(SDV)* or twenty SEALs. The *DDS* can safely survive the same depth as the submarine's test limit. U.S. Navy

Sea

- Selected *Los Angeles* class submarines are equipped with the capacity to carry a *SEAL Delivery Vehicle (SDV)*. The attack submarines can accommodate a single dry-deck shelter (DDS), which is capable of carrying a *SEAL Delivery Vehicle* or up to twenty SEALs. The older converted ballistic missile submarines (*USS King Kamehameha SSN-642)* can carry two dry-deck shelters. However, the *USS King* Kamehameha was decommissioned in June 2002. Two dry-deck shelters translate to up to forty

SEALs, or two *SDVs*. Converted Ohio class SSBNs will be used.

Dry-dock shelters (DDS) carry SEALs safely, as well as *SDVs*. A DDS is composed of a hyperbaric chamber, hangar, and access sphere. The value of a DDS lies in its capability to deliver its occupants, or SDV, to a target area without the rigors of swimming, cold, and fatigue. Conserving human strength for the mission is vital, and the trip to hostile territory should not sap the strength of the SEALs. A DDS can be attached to a submarine that has special fittings in about 12

The former ballistic missile submarine *USS Kamehameha SSN-642*, which was converted to carry dry-deck shelters *(DDS)* for special operations. The *Kamehameha* is an older *Benjamin Franklin* class Cold War deterrent ballistic missile submarine. At one time it sat with its Polaris missiles awaiting a call to launch them against Soviet military/industrial targets. Before being decommissioned in summer 2001 it played host to SEALs and their delivery units, and was based at Pearl Harbor. This venerable old boat is soon scheduled for nuclear recycling and scrapping. U.S. Navy

A helo appears over the twin dry deck shelters to unload supplies and men onto a slowly moving submarine. SEALs travel by any number of means to an objective. Helo to submarine to *SDV* to open ocean to walking and back! U.S. Navy

hours. Currently, the attack submarines *USS Los Angeles SSN-688, USS Philadelphia SSN-690, USS Dallas SSN-700, USS La Jolla SSN-701, USS Buffalo, USS Charlotte SSN-766, USS Greenville SSN-772, Virginia class SSN-774,* and the *Jimmy Carter SSN-21* class are slated to be equipped for existent Seal Delivery Vehicles and a new version being tested, the *Advanced Seal Delivery System (ASDS)*. The DDS are 38 feet in length and can be carried to the test depth of the attack submarine host. The DDS can be transportable to its host via any method, including by air.

The Seal Delivery Vehicle is a fiberglass "wet" boat that carries eight SEALs in a wet environment that requires individual breathing apparatus for each passenger. There are fifteen units that are powered by battery driven 18 hp electric motors. The pilot of the *SDV* is in the open, while the passengers are under a removable fiberglass cover. Riding in an SDV is cold and fatiguing. It is better than swimming, but is still difficult for the occupants. A new system is being tested at present (Advanced Seal Delivery System – ASDS) that is a closed mini-submarine. This will ultimately reduce the reliance on the open, or wet SDVs.

- A Combat Rubber Raiding Craft (CRRC) can be launched from a submarine, helicopter, Mark V Special Operations Craft, RIB, or conventional warship. It is a 15.4-foot long neoprene rubber Zodiak type boat that can be propelled by oars or one of two motors (35 hp or 55 hp). It carries up to eight SEALs, and can land ashore and then be hidden for extraction. It can also be used to drop SEALs

A SEAL Delivery Vehicle *(SDV)* being loaded for SEAL Team Two to carry out type training in the warm waters of the Caribbean. U.S. Navy

A *SDV* operator signals OK as the craft emerges from the dry-deck shelter aboard a host submarine. All of those that travel aboard contemporary *SDVs* use their own air supply. The *SDV* is just a cold wet method of moving men to an objective for them to swim out of and then to the work at hand. It does save wear and tear on the body and is a stealthy type method of arrival and departure. It is also tiring and cramped. U.S. Navy

SEALs work with combat rubber raiding craft (*CRRC*) on the aft part of a submarine. These boats can be inflated quickly and put over the side of a submarine in darkness with the SEAL squads and outboard motors in a matter of minutes. Author's collection.

A combat rubber raiding craft (*CRRC*) in front of the tailer that would carry it to an operating area for training purposes. In the background, two outboard motors that will be used with the CRRC can be seen, as well as the towing truck. Author's collection.

A fully inflated *CRRC* with its heavy duty Evinrude V4 outboard motor attached. For ease of launching during a training exercise, a simple boat trailer towed behind a pickup truck is used. Normally, a Boston Whaler surf boat stands by during deep water evolutions as a safety precaution. Author's Collection

1,000 or so meters from the shore (or whatever distance is considered appropriate) for them to swim in through the surf or into a harbor. (Scouts normally precede the main body to determine the "lay of the land," and then signal other SEALs to approach when it is safe).

- A specially equipped submarine can be employed to bring SEAL operators close to their objective for insertion and extraction. They can swim from the partially submerged boat ashore and be retrieved at a later time in the same fashion. This method entails a great deal of physical exertion and obvious fatigue for the SEALs.
- The *Mark V Special Operations Craft* can carry up to four combat rubber raiding craft and deliver them to within a reasonable distance from the objective. They can then retire at high speed to an over the horizon location to await a recall. The Mark V is transportable by amphibious vessels and by air (U.S. Air Force *C-5 Galaxy*)
- A Rigid Hulled Inflatable Boat (RIB) can be used, which has a range of 200 nautical miles and a top speed of over 40 knots. It is capable of carrying a SEAL squad of

Two outboard motors of choice. The SEALs use a 35 horsepower or a 55 horsepower outboard motor for the smaller craft. Motors have been accidentally dropped over the side in San Diego Bay, retrieved by a swimmer, and started up. They may look worn, but they are well maintained. Author's Collection

A *CRRC* is deployed out of a *CH-46E Sea Knight* helicopter by members of SEAL Team Eight at the U.S. Naval Academy (Annapolis). SEALs then followed in an insertion and extraction exercise. This was a "look-see" for naval academy midshipmen to entice them into the Naval Special Warfare community. This photo was taken on March 3, 2000, and the water must have been quite cold. No matter, SEALs are used to any and all conditions. U.S. Navy

The well at the stern of the *USS Monsoon PC-4*, which has been retro-fitted with a stern gate and well to deploy and recover special operations craft, including an 11 meter *RIB* and its crew and SEAL squad. To the starboard and trailing aft is a *Mark V SOC* coming alongside for refueling from the larger patrol craft. Both vessels can and are used for insertion and extraction of SEAL personnel. Courtesy George Bisharat

A *Mark V SOC* coming at speed toward the photographer. The *Mark V* can carry up to four *CRRCs* for SEAL insertion and extraction, and can be used in the same role to allow swimmers to deploy. Newer versions are more stealthy in appearance, but still stand out on sophisticated radar. U.S. Navy

eight men and delivering them to a target area. The 11 meter RIBs are faster, quieter, and deflect spray better than past models. They have two mounts (forward and aft) for fifty caliber machine guns and/or grenade launchers.

- The 170' 1/2" long *Coastal Patrol (PC)* boat can carry a detachment of nine special operations personnel. All are capable of launching and recovering combat rubber raid-

ing craft, and a small number of have been modified for carrying an 11 meter *RIB*. Although these craft are aesthetically attractive, they are not stealthy, nor have they lived up to the expectations of the naval special warfare community. The coastal patrol craft is not a delivery vehicle of choice when other means are available.

- Other amphibious warfare vessels, such as Amphibious Assault Ships (*Wasp class LHD, Tarawa class LHA, Austin*

An 11 meter *RIB* and its crew prepare to leave the Special Boat Squadron piers in Coronado, California, for an exercise in San Diego Bay in this January 2001 image. In the background the upper works of the patrol boat *USS Hurricane PC-3* can be seen. A *RIB* can tow two *CRRCs* to a launch or insertion point and retire at high speed over the horizon to any number of vessels equipped to retrieve it, including modified patrol boats like the *USS Monsoon PC-4*, sister to the *Hurricane*. Author's Collection

On January 11, 2000, SEAL parachutists exit from the rear of a *COD* (carrier on board delivery) *C-2 Greyhound* aircraft over Andersen Air Force Base on Guam. These are members of SEAL Team One that are conducting static line jumps as a means of insertion. U.S. Navy

class LPD, *Whidbey Island LSD, Anchorage class LSD*, and the new *San Antonio class LPD* being built by Northrop Grumman Litton Shipbuilding Systems). SEALs are also embarked in Carrier Battle Groups in the Atlantic and can respond from nuclear carriers, as well as from amphibious ships.

Air

- "Fast Roping" from a helicopter. The SEALs can use a variety of helicopters, including the *HH-60H "Seahawk,"* U.S. Air Force *MH-53J Pave Low*, and the *CH-46E Sea Knight*. The Navy has eleven active and two reserve squadrons of *Seahawk* helos that can be called upon for use in special operations. SEALs drop from their host rotary wing aircraft quickly into a landing zone (LZ), and then both rapidly fade away.

SEALs *"fast rope"* from a *SH-60H Seahawk* at Pearl Harbor. Members of SEAL Team one, Special Dive Unit and SEAL team Five (Golf platoon) repel from one of the helos attached to the *"Black Knights"* of Anti-Submarine Warfare Four. This exercise was a part of *RIMPAC 2000*, an annual multi-national naval exercise in the Pacific. U.S. Navy

SEALs demonstrate the use of the *SPIE (Special Purpose Insertion/ Extraction)* rig at Fort Pierce, Florida. Up to eight men can be swiftly and relatively safely inserted and extracted using a special parachute-like harness attached to an extended length of rope. In and out. Courtesy UDT/SEAL Museum

The parachute folding and rigging room at the U.S. Navy Special Warfare Center in Coronado, California. Author's Collection

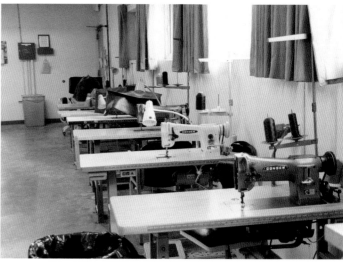

Heavy duty sewing machines used to repair parachutes and related rigging. The importance of exceptional repair work cannot be stressed enough. When a SEAL leaves a *C-130 Hercules,* helo, or *Greyhound COD,* he expects his chute to work. Author's Collection

- 30/30 Drop, or "helo casting." It is a misnomer that SEALs and their equipment jump thirty feet from the water's surface out the back door of a *Sea Knight* or any other helicopter moving forward at 30 knots. This may sound exciting, but the reality is ten feet and 15 knots. Men are preserved, and equipment, including combat rubber raiding craft, survive the fall and don't sink. Men can be retrieved via ladder hung down to the water's surface or *SPIE* rigging. The Special Purpose Insertion and Extraction *(SPIE)* rig is difficult and dangerous. This type of extraction can be done with a number of personnel on a long line dropped from the helo, and then with a quick surge fly upward and away from the extraction point. Similarly, a Stabilized Tactical Airborne Body Operation *(STABO)* extraction can be performed via a specialized

harness and quick connection to a hovering helo. This too is very dangerous and not generally utilized unless there are no other options.

- Helicopter insertion by landing at a deserted locale and then vanishing as quickly as possible and returning later for extraction when signaled or at a preplanned time and location.

- Parachute drops from helicopters or carrier on board delivery (COD) C-2A Greyhound aircraft. SEALs occasionally use a carrier based C-2A Greyhound aircraft for low altitude jumping. Special forces also use the *C-130 Hercules* for a High Altitude Low Altitude parachute opening *(HALO)*. SEALs exit the rear door of the aircraft at extreme altitudes (30,000 feet+) and free fall for several seconds before opening their parachutes at a low alti-

Parachute rigging in the SEAL Team One storage area at the U.S. Navy Special Warfare Center in Coronado, California. Author's Collection

Parachute rigging drying area outside of SEAL Team One's area in Coronado. Author's Collection

Parachute Loft from the ground looking upward at the Naval Special Warfare Center in Coronado. Author's Collection

tude. *HAHO* insertion is similar, except it is a High Altitude High Opening evolution. They then guide themselves to the intended landing spot using an *MC-1* canopy.

In some ways, the SEALs of today have much in common with 17th and 18th Century pirates. They sneak up on a target, secure it, achieve their goal, and leave. A major difference lies in the fact that they are the "good guys" and work for the United States government.

In any event, a SEAL and his team are pumped for an operation when a *Warning Order* comes down. Planning increases the adrenaline, and by the time the insertion begins most men are anxious, but ready. The work can be swift and easy or highly dangerous and fatiguing. When the work is done, SEALs do not come back to the fold in triumph—they are worn out, wet, and tired beyond all reason. They brief the command on the success or failure of the mission and then do what all ordinary men with extraordinary skills do—they rest and recuperate.

A *Greyhound COD* on board a nuclear carrier. This aircraft is used to insert SEALs by parachute to a designated area. The *COD* is also a workhorse for the fleet and brings everything from men and materials to mail to the carrier from land bases or other carriers at sea. U.S. Navy

A *CH-53E Sea Stallion* in a deserted sand pit in Bosnia with its occupants (SEALs) exiting the rear of the aircraft during a training exercise. U.S. Navy

An Amphibious Ready Group *(ARG)* led by the *USS Boxer LHD-4* in the Pacific. SEAL teams can deploy from any of the amphibious warships. U.S. Navy

An artist's conception of the new *San Antonio LPD-17* class of amphibious transport docks to be commissioned in 2003. The *LPD-17* class will be able to carry six transport helicopters and two *LCACs*. Provisions are being made to accommodate a SEAL team on this vessel and her sisters to come in the 21st century. Courtesy Northrop-Grumman Litton Shipbuilding

Chapter 6

Combat Crew and Special Boat Squadrons

Special Warfare Combat Crew - Background

In a sense the Special Warfare Combat Crew (SWCC), as they are now formally recognized in the U.S. Navy Special Warfare Community, can trace their heritage back as far as the beginning of the U.S. Navy. When armed seamen and marines came ashore to attack or seize a military or strategic objective, they were transported to and from frigates and sloops by launches manned by coxswains and boatmen. Often these men had to take command of a small boat howitzer or other weapons to ensure a safe extraction of men returning to the boats. The American Civil War added another dimension with the "riverine" style warfare up the bayous and

intricacies of the Mississippi River, and in and around the swamps and small islands adjacent to Confederate coastal areas.

This role of small boat operations came directly to light early in World War II with the 80' fast torpedo boats (*MTB*) used in Philippine waters and throughout the southwestern Pacific. These boats attacked Japanese shipping with torpedoes, carried guerillas, coast watchers, and supplies behind enemy lines, and generally raised havoc wherever possible. In another aspect entirely distinct from torpedo boat operations, there were small boat personnel used in every amphibious landing in the Pacific, Mediterranean, and Atlantic. Boat

One of the early pre-World War II 70' *Elco* motor torpedo boats *(MTB)* that when faced with combat were changed to reflect actual battle conditions. These boats could make over 40 knots and were armed with four 18" torpedoes and two twin fifty caliber machine guns. This was *PT-10*, and a later 80' version of the Elco *MTB* was commanded by then Lt jg John F Kennedy. His boat was *PT-109* and was lost in enemy action in the southwest Pacific. He later went on to become President of the United States, but never forgot his tour of duty as a PT skipper. *PT-10* and its successors were direct descendents of the Combat Crew and SEALs. Author's Collection

A lone *PBR* of the Riverine Forces in the Mekong Delta makes its way to an operation in mid river. The chances of being hit by enemy fire from the river banks was least in the middle of the river. The *PBRs* often worked at night, especially when ferrying SEALs, other special forces personnel, or CIA operatives. Courtesy Len Swiatly

The *USS Jennings County LST 846* anchored in a South Vietnamese River. The *Jennings County* was no stranger to Vietnam, having participated in operation "Passage to Freedom" when she assisted in the evacuation of thousands of Vietnamese nationals from North Vietnam after the French defeat in 1955. The World War II built *LST* acted as a station ship and base for *PBRs* and other special operations craft during the Vietnam War and was actively involved in *Operation Game Warden*. Courtesy Len Swiatly

A group of Combat Crew (*Special Boat Unit 12 – RIB*) on a pier at the Special Warfare Center in Coronado, California, in late January 2001. From left to right are SM2 Caldwell, Lt (jg) Rehberg, OS2 Norton, ITSN Payne, and IC2 Ojinaga. These men are about to take out two of the 11 meter *RIBs* on a training exercise and are all combat crew qualified. They have 21st century equipment and training, yet have much in common with *MTB* sailors of the early 1940s and "brown water" sailors of the 1960s and 1970s. Author's Collection

captains of wooden landing craft *(LCVPs)* took wave after wave of soldiers and marines to a hostile beachhead with their own personal defense being a lightly protected .30 caliber machine gun, Douglas fir planking, and the dungarees they wore. Five years after the end of World War II, the same landing craft were again crewed by men taking their charges ashore in Korean waters.

The role of the Combat Crew of today came into full focus during the war fought in the deltas and rivers of South Vietnam during the late 1960s and early 1970s. Here they emerged as a navy within a navy and established a direct

linkage to another new kid on the block—the SEALs. The "Brown Water Navy," or "Riverine Forces" as they became known, racked up an incredible string of successes in the muggy, muddy, insect ridden backwaters of the Mekong Delta and swamp areas. Eventually, they had over 38,000 personnel and over 700 craft that were designed or invented on the spot for their type of warfare.

It began in 1965, and two years later, on January 30, 1967, formal recognition was given when the Naval Inshore Operations Training Center was established at the Mare Island Naval Shipyard in Vallejo, California. Crewmen were

A *Cyclone* class coastal patrol boat at speed and in an early camouflage scheme. Looking closely, the forward and aft Mark 38 25mm weapons can be seen, as well as the fifty caliber machine guns on the bridge wings. A six meter *RIB* is stowed aft on the port side with a small crane for launch and recovery. Several of the class have now been modified to accommodate a *RIB* in a stern well with a gate that closes behind. The retrofitted patrol craft are nine feet longer than the original 170' length of the *Cyclone* class. They are beautiful vessels at high speed. U.S. Navy taught the ways of river and delta warfare in the muddy waters of the Sacramento Delta region and the Napa River that flows right between Mare Island and the City of Vallejo.

The Navy realized that, except for shore bombardment by destroyers and cruisers and air strikes from carriers, much of the naval war would be fought on brown water rather than at sea. Three task forces were established to accommodate this new type of warfare. *Task Force 117* was established as a river assault force, while *Task Force 116* was assigned river patrol and surveillance and *Task Force 115* was designed to patrol the coastline. All were used to combat the flow of men and supplies to South Vietnam through the thousands of miles of river waterways. The Air Force and Navy were bombarding overland supply routes, but waterways were the responsibility of the navy and its riverine forces. For endless months the "brown water" navy, including the SEALs, fought a tide of Viet Cong and North Vietnamese operatives and regulars, and did an admirable job of reducing the flood of supplies and equipment. As the war wound down for the American Forces, the brown water navy and the SEALs became advisors to the Vietnamese Navy, who gradually assumed control of all riverine craft left in South Vietnam. Unfortunately, by 1975 it was evident that the cause was lost, and North Vietnam overran the South, capturing all of the boats and watercraft left behind under the "Vietnamization" plan.

A passageway or catwalk across the three separate superstructure housings aboard the *Hurricane*. To the left are ready ammunition boxes for *Stinger* missiles, and just straight ahead is the ship's brass bell. Like all naval vessels, the decks are covered with a non-skid substance to reduce falls and injury. Author's Collection

The bridge of the *USS Hurricane PC-3*. The engine controls are to the right and the wheel is in the center of the image. The bridge area is small and literally jammed with electronic equipment. Author's Collection

The bow and forward part of the *USS Hurricane PC-3* based at Coronado, California, in late January 2001. A sailor is at work painting the forward hull of the ship and the sole anchor that is connected to a chain leading into the forepeak. A week earlier a sister ship, the *USS Monsoon PC-4*, was taking green water over her bow during a storm at sea while transiting from Astoria, Oregon, to San Francisco, California. Author's Collection

For the thirteen years after the conclusion of the Vietnam War the Riverine Forces continued to operate, but on a reduced scale. In 1983, the existing boat support units were reorganized into Special Boat Units, and in 1987 were integrated into U.S. Navy Special Warfare with the SEAL Teams and Seal Delivery Vehicle (SDV) Teams. In 2001, the organization now includes Special Boat Squadron I based out of Coronado, California, and Special Boat Squadron 2 based out of Little Creek, Virginia. There are also Special Boat Detachments located in various part of the United States, and a large reserve organization of Combat Crew and various boat types. Like the SEALs, the Special Warfare Combat Crew and their craft have grown and become allied into one large organization. Recently, the Special Warfare Combat Crew (SWCC) became formally recognized for their skills, and after a rigorous training program are awarded an appropriate insignia and designation. No longer are they Surface Warfare sailors that operate craft for the SEALs. This is for enlisted personnel. Surface Warfare rated commissioned officers command at the unit and group levels, as well as the *Cyclone* class patrol boats.

Surface Warfare Combat Crew (SWCC) - Enlisted

With the new designation as a Combat Crewmember, recruiting and training programs already in existence have been formalized as well. Recruits come from a number of sources, but must have at least two years left in active service after SWCC training and pass a rigorous physical and aptitude test to make it into SWCC training. Candidates must be men, have 20/20 correctable vision, be 30 years or less in age, and be qualified as a "second class" swimmer or better to be accepted (a waiver of two years in age is possible).

The physical screening test includes timed distance swimming and other tests to determine strength and endurance. If a candidate passes through this screening and then makes it into the program he is warned to get his personal affairs in order. Training is seven days a week for ten weeks at the Naval Special Warfare Center in Coronado, California.

The training is laid out on a week by week basis, and by the end of week nine, a candidate must be able to make a 1,000 yard swim in full uniform in less than 30 minutes. In addition, he must complete a four mile run in sand in full uniform (including boots) in 38 minutes, and aside from other physical tests, make a one mile ocean swim with fins in fifty or less minutes.

The aft part of the *Hurricane*, which shows the six-meter *RIB* and the crane for launching and recovery of the boat. On the starboard side aft is a mount for a machine gun, but its is stored below out of the elements. Author's Collection

Lt. Patrick Blake of the Supply Corps demonstrates the scarf ring within which a combat crewmember steadies himself to fire a hand held *Stinger* missile aboard the *USS Hurricane*. The *Stinger FM-92* model has a range of 3 miles, and the high explosive warhead carrying missile is guided by infrared homing. It is quite effective against small boats and low flying rotary wing aircraft. Author's Collection

The step area and entry/exit hatch for SEALs to board and leave the *RIB* as it comes up to the stern of the *Hurricane*. This system has proven unwieldy and cumbersome. It also exposes the SEALs and combat crewmen to enemy fire for an inordinate amount of time when time is of the essence. Author's Collection

The trainees are taught the basics for the operation of a combat rubber raiding craft, Mark V SOC, Rigid Hulled Inflatable Boats (RIB), and other craft within the Navy Special Warfare inventory. They learn comprehensive first aid, maritime navigation including long range voyage planning, seamanship, and engineering skills. The Combat Crew has to know how to repair a jet drive, ensure that the engines run cool, and when the hull, engine, or electronics are damaged

by enemy fire, how to quickly repair the damage. Aside from learning the technical ins and outs of each boat type, they also maintain the equipment. There may come a time like their forefathers that they have to fight and defend themselves as well as their passengers, and this calls for warfare and weapon skills. They do not put to sea without their own personal weapons, and like the SEALs are prepared to meet an enemy. They are not just boat drivers.

At the end of ten hard weeks, the surviving candidates graduate and transfer for an additional year to meet the qualifications required for a SWCC insignia. Part and parcel to this element of their training is assignment to a boat and a squadron. It is there that they begin another phase of learning—on the job. The boats become part of their lives, and they take great pride in the boat's appearance and its fitness to operate. They are also given a higher degree of responsibility than those with similar ratings in the "big ship" navy. The adoption of the SWCC program, along with specialized training and a separate rating, is hoped to maintain a trained force of men. For a commissioned officer, being assigned to a boat squadron or one of the *Cyclone* class patrol boats provides priceless command experience and is one the few slots in the Navy where a junior officer is given so much responsibility and latitude of action. The cyclone class remains crewed with Surface Warfare personnel with a SWCC liaison.

Overall, the Combat Crew and the officers who lead them have come a long way from the early days of fighting destroyers from plywood boats and sparring with rockets, mines, and machine gun fire nightly in the mud and filth of the Mekong Delta. Their spirit remains unchanged, but the equipment has.

The stabilized Mark 38 25mm 87 caliber *Bushmaster* aft on the *USS Monsoon PC-4*. The *Bushmaster* is capable of firing a 1.1 pound projectile up to 2,500 yards at a rate of a single shot, or up to 200 round per minute. The *Cyclone* class *PCs* are the only vessels in the U.S. arsenal with permanent mounts for the *Bushmaster*. It has been used on other ships that are being deployed to high threat regions where small attack craft may be encountered. Courtesy George Bisharat

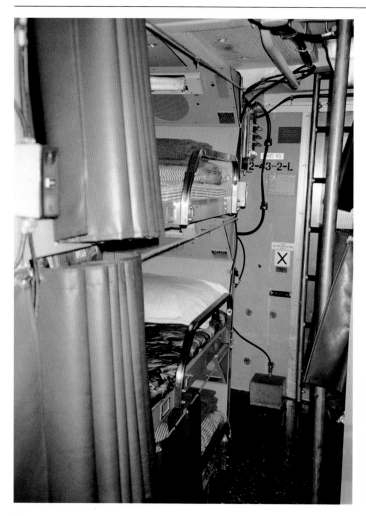

Three tiered bunks aboard the *USS Hurricane* for Combat Crew or guests. The green curtains are for privacy, not that there is any aboard these ships. The 30 men who live aboard these vessels must be amiable and get along well together for the ship to succeed. When SEALs are embarked the total is 39, and a proper attitude often stands between orderliness and chaos. Author's Collection

A Combat Crewmember aboard the *Hurricane* takes time out to work on his laptop personal computer. He is dressed in a flight suit, which seems to be the clothing of choice for many of the crew. Flight suits are rugged, warm, and easy to wear. This individual is in the mess hall, and the term is used loosely. Author's Collection

Small area of storage for Combat Crew's uniforms and wet suit. The amount of space allowed each crew member and each officer is not much different—both have very little. The *Cyclone* class ships were designed for 10 day or less operations and not for the comfort of the crew. Author's Collection

The Craft of U.S. Navy Special Warfare

Cyclone Class Coastal Patrol Vessels

The most high profile craft in special warfare is the *Cyclone* class *PC*, or coastal patrol vessel. Since the namesake of the class (*USS Cyclone PC-1*) was commissioned on August 7, 1993, she has been followed by thirteen other ships. The last was the *USS Tornado PC-14*, commissioned on June 24, 2000. All were built by the Bollinger Shipyards in Lockport, Louisiana.

The class is 170.5' in length with a beam of 25 feet, and displaces 331 tons full load. They are powered by four Paxman Valenta diesels generating 13,400 bhp. The engines are connected to four shafts that turn six blade propellers, and the only other vessels in the navy with four propellers are the fossil fuel and nuclear powered aircraft carriers. The *Cyclone* class can make up to 35 knots and has a 3,000 nautical mile range at 12 knots with a 18,600 gallon diesel fuel tank. The hull is made of steel, and the superstructure out of aluminum.

The galley aboard the *Hurricane*. There is a stove range, and as can be seen, the central piece of cooking equipment is a microwave oven. The Crew know how to clean up after they have used the galley—there is no maid service. The food is like that served on most naval vessels, with emphasis on ease of storage and preparation. Author's Collection

Aft near the hatch leading to the well deck where a RIB would be retrieved by crane on the *Hurricane*. A portable body transport board replete with emergency medical equipment is available to provide aid to the injured and save lives. Sailors assigned to PCs are trained in first aid far beyond any other sailors, except corpsmen. When a wounded half frozen SEAL comes back aboard, the difference in life or death rests with the equipment available and the skills of a well trained Combat Crew. Author's Collection

A *Mark V SOC* with single and twin 50 caliber machine guns manned and ready. The aft ramp is used to recover *CRRCs* or smaller *RIBs*. The *Mark V* has an aluminum hull, and can race at speeds over 50 knots. They are excellent boats for insertion/extraction of up to a platoon of SEALs. U.S. Navy

There is some armor in the form of one inch thick applique on selected areas of the superstructure, but this is only to afford minor protection against small arms fire.

The ship's complement includes four officers and 24 enlisted men. Unlike many other naval vessels, senior enlisted personnel who are "officer of the deck" qualified can stand bridge watches. There are simply not enough officers to carry out "big ship" protocol.

The *Cyclone* class carries up to nine SEALs or special operations personnel, yet can embark more in an emergency. During the 1994 Haitian relief expedition, twenty-five SEALs were crammed aboard each of the four PCs assigned to the operation. Unfortunately, the *Cyclone* class does not provide more than the bare necessities for living, but for Naval Special Warfare personnel, it is far preferable to being cold and wet.

The PCs are armed with a variety of weapons, including two Mark 38 25mm/87 caliber guns (*Bushmaster or chain guns*), of which one is unstabilized forward, yet the aft weapon is stabilized for greater accuracy. 2,000 rounds of ammunition are normally carried for these weapons. In addition to the 25mm guns, there is a simple scarf ring *Stinger FM-92* missile position, two fifty caliber guns, two 40mm grenade launchers, and two M-60, 7.62mm machine guns. There are also numerous small arms for the crew and its passengers.

This class of patrol craft also carries state of the art radar and detection systems, including a bridge sited Forward Looking Infrared (*FLIR*) system, and is also equipped with numerous communication systems.

Overall, there are mixed reviews about the suitability of the *Cyclone* class for the tasks envisioned, and some feel that too many compromises based on maximizing cost effectiveness have literally shortchanged the *PCs* from their intended roles. They have performed well in every theater assigned, but in a heavy sea state they tend to suffer, and the clutter of their superstructures provides a well defined enemy radar signature.

One area that has been rectified is the ability of some of the vessels to launch and retrieve an 11 meter *RIB*. As originally designed, the class was able to launch and recover a single six meter *RIB*, yet in the case of *Tornado PC-14, Shamal PC-13, Zephyr PC-8, Tempest PC-2*, and *Monsoon PC-4*, the stern has been retrofitted to accommodate a full size *RIB*. These vessels have been extended nine feet, and the original step in the stern counter has been removed to allow for a well and gate. Now known as the *Tempest* class, this extension will enable retrieval more quickly, and thus exposure to enemy fire will be reduced.

The *USS Cyclone* has been transferred to the U.S. Coast Guard for illegal drug suppression and interdiction missions. This is a perfect role for this type of vessel. As of October 2001 six cyclone class PCs were transferred to Homeland Defense for harbor patrol. Those with the stern conversion will remain with Naval Special Warfare.

A *Mark V* is being loaded aboard an Air Force Reserve *C-5 Galaxy* for a trip to an unknown destination. The boat, its trailer, and other vehicles, plus ammunition and communications equipment, are also transported in a like fashion, and a SEAL team can be inserted with this craft anywhere in the world in less than three days. U.S. Navy

A *CRRC* with its outboard motor is loaded aboard a *MARK V*. It is being readied for a training exercise in late January 2001 at the Naval Special Warfare Center at Coronado, California. Just forward of the inflated boat is a deflated *CRRC*. Author's Collection

Cushioned seats with head rests for sixteen passengers aboard a *MARK V*. Although the occupants have seats and under cover, the ride is rough and hard. Of course, that is what the SEALs have trained for. Once close to a target area, a *CRRC* or *CRRCs* will be launched for a trip ashore or close (800-1,500 yards) ashore. Author's Collection

Mark V Special Operations Craft (SOC)

The 75 ton full load *Mark V SOC* is relatively new to naval special warfare, the first two having entered the inventory in 1995 and the last of twenty ordered in the year 2000. They are built by Trinity-Halter Marine based in Gulfport, Mississippi, and are 82' in length with a 17' beam. The hull and superstructure are made of aluminum, and they are powered by two diesel engines generating 2,285 horsepower. The diesel engines drive two waterjets, and the *Mark Vs* have a top speed of over 50 knots with a range of 600 nautical miles.

These boats are highly maneuverable, but they too suffer in any heavy sea state. They are not designed to remain at sea for long periods of time and are used for single mission purposes. They do have cover for their crew and passengers from the elements, and the seats are heavily padded to absorb the punishment of an aluminum boat pounding its way through the swells or an ocean chop.

The *Mark V* is crewed by five Combat Crew (commanding officer is a leading petty officer), and the boats are armed with two twin fifty caliber machine guns, two single fifty cali-

A photo taken through the plastic windows on the starboard side reveals a whole arsenal of small arms that will employed by the Combat Crew and/or their passengers. Author's Collection

A close up look at a twin fifty caliber machine gun and its mounting. The gun barrel and ammunition are stored until the need arises. There are also positions for M-60 7.62 caliber machine guns and a 40mm grenade launcher, as well as a limited number of *Stinger* missiles. A deflated *CRRC* and partially dismantled outboard motor can be seen on the deck, and in the background a *Mark V* that has been retrofitted with a new mast for radar and other electronic antennas. The new mast will become standard, as it reduces the radar signature of the boat. Author's Collection

Flying the American flag, a *Mark V* makes its way out into San Diego Bay. All of its weapons are assembled on their mounts, and the boat will exercising at sea during the night. Most of the *Mark Vs* are painted in various camouflage patterns dependent on what area of the world they will be working in. Author's Collection

ber weapons, and grenade launchers and positions for M-60 machine guns. Their primary armament lies in the ability to carry a full SEAL platoon of sixteen men. These boats can come up over the horizon at high speed and towing one or two *RIBs* to release them for further operations. The *Mark Vs* can also carry four *CRRCs* for inshore attack.

One of the most attractive features of these boats is their air and vessel portability. They can be carried aboard any amphibious craft, but more importantly, can be transported aboard a U.S. Air Force *C-5 Galaxy*. When a crisis situation arises, a *Mark V* or *Mark Vs* can be transported, along with its six support vehicles, ammunition supplies, and onshore command and control station aboard the USAF *C-5s*. This allows a SEAL platoon and a high speed insertion/extraction

vehicle to be anywhere in the world with 48 hours. This can be critical in a rapidly deteriorating political or diplomatic situation. Overall, the SEALs and Combat Crew are pleased with this addition to their fleet of vessels.

11 Meter Rigid Hulled Inflatable Boat (RIB)

The *RIB* is 11 meters in length and has a beam of 10" 8". It displaces nine tons, and is capable of carrying a Squad of eight fully equipped SEALs and three crew. The boats are commanded by a leading petty officer among the three Combat Crew.

The hull is made of fiberglass with a kevlar reinforced resin. It is a "deep V" hull that has two piece nylon reinforced neoprene sponsons that reduce spray and help maintain sea

The 11 meter *Rigid Inflatable Boat (RIB)* at high speed with its crew but no passengers. Both single barrel .50 caliber guns are visible (aft and forward). They are for protecting their craft and SEALs that are embarking after a mission. U.S. Navy

Aboard a 11 meter *RIB*, a Combat Crewmember driver looks over his shoulder to watch the terrain. One of the crew is manning the aft .50 caliber machine gun, and just forward of the gunner, a body board can be seen lashed to empty seats. Also seen are the seats and railing that a SEAL squad use when traveling at high speed and a very bumpy ride. The neoprene sponsons that surround the deep V hull are not for floatation, but help stabilize the boat and reduce the amount of sea spray coming aboard. U.S. Navy

The driver's console of a 11 meter *RIB*. The engine and steering controls are obvious, and the many indicators show engine temperature, fuel levels, and power being used. The 11 meter *RIB* comes with VHF/UHF communications systems, night vision equipment, and a Global Positioning System (*GPS*), as well as a depth finder. These two RIBs have their main mast and "radar pot" forward of the console, yet others may have them closer to the stern. Author's Collection

Two 11 meter *RIBs* and crews from *Special Boat Unit 12* prepare to leave the dock in January 2001 for a training exercise outside San Diego Bay. Both boats carry radar and sophisticated electronic equipment. The *RIBs* are driven by waterjets connected to twin turbo charged diesels. Author's Collection

Chapter 6: Combat Crew and Special Boat Squadrons 71

Forward .50 caliber machine gun and mount aboard a 11 meter *RIB*. Author's Collection

Aft sited .50 caliber machine gun and mount on a 11 meter *RIB*. Two radio antennas flank the weapon, and the gun mount doubles as a king post for securing lines. Author's Collection

Combat Crewmember Norton, assigned to one of the *RIBs* of *Special Boat Unit 12*, shows the front of his vest. Each mission calls for different equipment, but in the main, this vest would normally contain: first aid kit; compass; knife; chemical lights; survival radio; ammunition; and goggles. During an operation, it is vital for all members of the crew and the SEALs to know where specific items are located in case of an emergency. For this reason, the location of critical items is known to all. A Combat Crewmember's life may depend on one of the other crew being able to find his first aid kit. Author's Collection

The back of the vest includes some of the major items, but also flexible fins, and a holster for the crewmember's weapon is seen on the right hip. The weapon is that of choice, but is generally a .45 caliber Mark 23 special application handgun, or "cannon." Author's Collection

An 11 meter *RIB* makes speed with SEALs riding on the sponson as part of a demonstration in San Diego Bay. This is a form of SEAL insertion. U.S. Navy

A *PBR* on riverine exercise in the Sacramento Delta area. The *PBRs* are still used for Naval Special Warfare, but have been generally relegated to the backwaters of operations. George Bisharat

keeping. The boats are powered by two Caterpillar turbo charged diesels that together generate 940 horsepower. They are capable of a top speed of 47 knots and a range of 200 nautical miles.

The *RIB* employs a small radar set, depth finder, and a GPS. Its communications suite includes marine band, tactical, VHF/UHF, and satellite communications. All bands are capable of ciphering and deciphering. The boat can be armed with a fifty caliber machine gun forward and one aft, as well as a 40mm grenade launcher. This is in addition to the weapons carried by the Combat Crew and their passengers. In all, the RIB is a potent and well designed insertion/extraction vehicle. Much of its success is based on the fact that it was designed with the input of naval special warfare personnel, including those who would operate them.

Aside from Combat Crew, the 11 meter *RIB* is also utilized by other elements of the Navy and the U.S. Coast Guard. It is a very popular vessel that has a wide range of applications.

PBRs/Armoured Troop Carriers/Other Patrol Craft

Naval Special Warfare also employs craft that date back to the Vietnam War, including the Riverine Patrol Boats (*PBR*) of the Mark 2 type and the Armoured Troop Carriers (*Mini ATC*). The *PBR* is a 8.9 ton full load craft that is 32' in length with a 12' beam. It is the craft most heavily associated with the "brown water" navy of the Vietnam War. Over 500 were built during the period 1965-1974, and many were lost when the North Vietnamese military overran the South in 1975. Several remained in the United States, and a few were built during the 1980s. At this point, these tried and true boats are assigned to Reserve detachments. They were powered by diesel engines and could make up to 24 knots on twin waterjet propulsion units. They were/are armed with differing weapons suites, including a 60mm mortar, Mark 38 25 mm *Bushmaster* cannon, a single 50 caliber machine gun, and a forty mm grenade launcher. This was in addition to the personal weapons of the four or five man crews.

What made the dark green *PBRs* so effective was their ability to get into and out of trouble quickly due to their ability

Another smaller riverine light patrol boat driven by four outboard motors, yet carrying radar and a mount for a machine gun up forward. This photo was taken in the Sacramento Delta, which has been a training ground for Combat Crew and SEALs for decades. George Bisharat

A light patrol boat (*PBL*) moves swiftly down into San Diego Bay abreast of the North Island Naval Air Station in early 1998. These boats are based on the Boston Whaler design and are driven by two outboard engines at a top speed of over 30 knots. They can be heavily armed with machine guns and grenade launchers and make ideal harbor security craft. Author's Collection

to maneuver in tight spots. They could literally stop and turn on a dime, and in the sloughs and bends of the Mekong Delta and other rivers, this was critical. Only a fraction of the original boats remain, including one at the memorial site at the U.S. Navy Amphibious Base in Coronado, California.

The armored troop carriers (*MATC*) also exist in small numbers, yet were built between 1972-1979. They are 36' in length with a 13'beam and displace nearly 15 tons full load. They can carry up to sixteen passengers and are crewed by three or four enlisted men. They have a top speed of over 25 knots and can carry two tons of cargo. Interestingly, they have a one foot draft at top speed with a full load. The Mini Armored Troop Carriers can be armed with seven heavy machine guns and grenade launchers, and their aluminum hulls are augmented with ceramic armor to afford some degree of protection to its occupants and cargo. There are 21 *MATCs* in the Naval Special Warfare inventory.

Other craft in the special warfare fleet include the 15' Combat Rubber Raiding Craft (*CRRC*), Light Patrol Boats (*PBL*), which are likened to Boston Whalers, and 40' High Speed Boats (*HSB*), which resemble cigarette boats yet can be heavily armed for insertion/extraction missions. The High Speed Boats are capable of speeds in excess of 55 knots, are for short duration missions, and can be transported in a USAF *C-5 Galaxy* or *C-141 Starlifter* transport aircraft.

The entire spectrum of Special Warfare support vessels has come quite a distance from the early days, as have the personnel who maintain and drive them. Now there are specialized boats for specialized tasks, and the men are rated as Combat Crew after a rigorous and combat focused training program. Along with the expansion of the SEALs, the Special Warfare Craft and Combat Crew testify to the value of U.S. Navy Special Warfare in the American military arsenal.

The newly designed and approved Combat Crewmember (or SWCC - Special Warfare Combat Crewmember) pin, which became available for those that have been fully trained as Combat Crewmembers. The pin, which has been awarded since summer 2001 to a limited number of naval special warfare personnel, will become standard after successfully passing a rigorous training program and a one year probationary period on the job. U.S. Navy.

A 25 mm/87 caliber Mark 38 *Bushmaster* rapid fire cannon. This is the main armament of the *Cyclone/Tempest* class *PC*s. This particular mount is shown aboard the *USS Ticonderoga* (CG-47), and is used throughout the U.S. military on other vessels, as well as the U.S. Army's Bradley AFV (Armored Fighting Vehicle). Over 10,000 of these cannon have been manufactured, and can put out a devastating fire at 200 rounds per minute. The *Cyclone/Tempest* class have fixed mounts for the weapon, whereas other warships have temporary installations so that the Mark 38 can be furnished to defend against small craft in high threat areas. U.S. Navy.

An aft view of a *Mark V SOC*, which clearly shows the four station fifty caliber gun armament, but moreover, the ramp upon which a *CRRC* can be retrieved while the *Mark V* is underway. The basic idea is to spend as little time during the vulnerable period of launch and retrieval of SEALs and other special operations personnel. Get in, get out, quietly and fast! Author's Collection.

Epilogue

From their rudimentary beginning and often threatened existence by those in the "traditional" military hierarchy, U.S. Navy Special Warfare has had a rough ride through the rocks and shoals of organization, funding, and recognition. It is safe to say now that they have earned themselves a place at the table when it comes to deciding national defense policy. The SEALs and Combat Crew are recognized inside and outside the American military as the finest weapon in its waterborne arsenal.

With its future relatively secure, it is obvious that Naval Special Warfare will be called upon for a great number of tasks as the United States and its allies makes their way through the uncertain times that lay ahead. During the Cold War, there was an identifiable enemy in the form of the now defunct Soviet Union. In the early 21st century, a great deal of time is spent looking over our shoulders to determine where a new enemy is coming from. There are also emerging third world nations that could irresponsibly begin a nuclear war, and terrorism is on the rise both domestically and abroad. On September 11, 2001, foreign terrorism of the most sinister and violent nature was visited upon innocent men, women, and children of the United States. The death toll is between 5,500 and 6,500 souls at last count, or four times the number lost on the *Titanic* in 1912. It will likely be the responsibility of Special Operations, including SEALs, to locate and destroy these well hidden and politically protected enemies. Another issue that Naval Special Warfare is concerned with is the suppression of illegal drugs from Central and South America into the United States. American destroyers, cruisers, frigates, and patrol boats with special warfare men and equipment are currently and will continue to be assigned to the Caribbean and eastern Pacific oceans. Much of the detection and other electronic equipment now available has been added to fast moving small surface craft *(RIBs)* to be used by trained men that spell doom to drug smugglers that use the waterways. Protecting the shores of the United States from cocaine and other drugs is as important as defeating other forms of terrorism to our citizens. Naval Special Warfare is expected to assume a greater role in this area of operations in the early 21st century.

Although there is great solace knowing that the United States is the most powerful nation in the world and perhaps in world history, our technologically dominant military cannot solve all problems everywhere and all of the time. Important issues can, however, be resolved by a clandestine force of highly trained men in the form of the U.S. Navy SEALs and Combat Crew. Problems that are inappropriate for an amphibious ready group *(ARG)* or carrier battle group *(CBG)* will increasingly be laid at the feet of the U.S. Special Operation Command *(USSOCOM)* and Naval Special Warfare. Improved technology, more stealthy equipment, such as small high speed surface craft with a low radar/heat signature, and the use of submersibles such as the *Advanced Seal Delivery System (ASDS)* will enable the SEALs and Combat Crew to do their job quicker and with greater safety.

Our known and potential enemies know that like a smart bomb or a *Tomahawk* missile, anywhere they go or hide they are susceptible to an attack by the best combat force in the world. That force will go in, do its job, and leave, and as always, will be *"the quiet professionals."*

Bibliography

I. Primary Materials

A. Private Papers - Manuscript/Photo Files
    Bonner, Kermit H Jr. - various
    Swiatly, Ken - various
B. Special Collections - Manuscript/Photo Collections
    Call Bulletin Newspaper Photo File, 1994, Treasure Island Museum - various
    Navy League of the United States, 2000
    Swiatly, Ken Vietnam War, Riverine Forces
    Treasure Island Museum Photo Files, 1994 – various
    United States Naval Institute, 1945 -2001 - various
    U.S. Navy, CHINFO Still Image Center
    U.S. Navy, Naval Special Warfare Command
    U.S. Navy, Naval Special Warfare Training Center

C. Interviews
    Alderson, J, Commander, USN – Public Affairs Officer NSW (Command)
    Blake, Patrick, Lt USN, SC
    Crawford, Don – Historian, U.S. Navy Special Warfare
    Licup, Katie, Lt. USN – Assistant Public Affairs Officer, NSW (Command) - Training
    McCabe, Tamsen, Lt USN - Public Affairs Officer, NSW (Center)
    O'Connor, Patricia, Public Affairs Office, NSW (Command)
    Pence, Petty Officer, USN, NSW
    Rehberg, LT (jg), Special Boat Squadron 1, SBU-12
    Wilkins, Andy, USN, NSW
    Witsotzki, Steve, LCDR, USN, BUD/S Training

D   U.S. Government Documents
    Naval Special Warfare Brochure
    Naval Special Warfare, U.S. Navy Seals – Fact File
    Special Boat Squadron One – Coronado, California
    United States Special Operations Command (10th Anniversary Issue), 1997
    "Full Mission Profile," Spring 1994, Winter 1994-1995, Winter 1995 -1996, Winter1996, Bulletins of Navy Special Warfare Command

II. Secondary Materials

A. Books, Monographs, Treaties

Sweetman, Jack, "American Naval History," Naval Institute Press, 1984

Staff Written, "Bluejackets Manual," U.S. Naval Institute, 1950

Cutler, Thomas J, "Brown Water, Black Berets," Naval Institute Press, 1988

Bonner, Kit & Carolyn "Cold War at Sea," MBI, 2000

Dwyer, John B, "Commandos from the Sea," Paladin Press, 1998

Office of Naval History, U.S. Navy, "Dictionary of American Naval Fighting Ship," all volumes, U.S. Government Printing Office, 1969

Bonner, Kit, "Final Voyages," Turner Publishing, 1996, 1999

Morison, Samuel Elliott, "History of United States Naval Operations in World War II," all volumes, Atlantic Little Brown and Co, 1962

Morris, James M., "History of the U.S. Navy," Brompton Books, 1993

Stubblefield, Gary & Halberstadt, Hans, "Inside the U.S. Navy Seals," MBI, 1995

Moore, J E, Editor, "Jane's Fighting Ships, 1986-87," Jane's Publishing Company, 1987

Blackman, Raymond, Editor, "Jane's Fighting Ships, 1968-1969," Jane's Publishing Group, 1970

Baker A D III, "The Naval Institute Guide to Combat Fleets of the World 2000-2001," Naval Institute Press, 2000

Polmar, Norman, "The Naval Institute Guide to the Ships and Aircraft of the U.S. Fleet," Naval Institute Press, 2001

Chant, Christopher, "Sea Forces of the World," Crescent Books, 1990

Humble, Richard, "Submarines, The Illustrated History," Basinghall Books Limited, 1981

Moore, John R. Captain RN, "The Soviet Navy Today," Stein and Day, 1975

Miller, Nathan, "The U.S. Navy, An Illustrated History," American Heritage Publishing Co., 1977

Landau, Alan M., Landau, Frieda M, Griswold, Giangreco, Halberstadt, Hans, "U S Special Forces," Lowe & B Hould Publishers, 1999

First Shot Naval Veterans, "USS Ward DD-139," Naval Veterans Co., 1986

Silverstone, Paul H., "U S Warships Since 1945," Naval Institute Press, 1987

Reilly, John, "United States Navy Destroyers of World War II," Blandford Press, 1983

Friedman, Norman, "U S Destroyers," Naval Institute Press, 1982

Friedman, "U S Cruisers," Naval Institute Press, 1984

Miller, Nathan, "U S Navy, an Illustrated History," American Heritage Publishing Co, Inc., 1977

Halberstadt, Hans, "U S Navy Seals in Action, MBI, 1995

Moeser, Robert D., "U S Navy: Vietnam," Naval Institute Press, 1969

Friedman, Norman, "U S Naval Weapons," Naval Institute Press," 1985

Friedman, Norman, "U S Small Combatants," Naval Institute Press, 1987

B. Articles

Loefstedt, Robert E, Lt USN, "The Brown Water Navy Lives," Full Mission Profile, Spring 1994

Himmelspach, Darlene, "Changes in SEAL Hell Week Follow Death of Trainee," Navy Times, June 18, 2001

Valentine, Dean, Lt USN, "SEAL Officers on Combatant Craft," Full Mission Profile, Spring 1994

Barrett, Steve, Sgt. 1st Class, USA, "Special Operations Commander Speaks of Changes Before Congress," Full Mission Profile, Spring 1994

Huff, Tim, Lt USN, "Surface Warfare Officers Assigned to Special Boat Units," Full Mission Profile, Spring 1994

McConnell, Malcolm, "The Toughest School on Earth," Readers Digest, August 1999

Olson, Eric T, Rear Admiral, USN, "Waterborne Commandos," Armed Forces Journal International, January 2000

C. Unpublished Works

SOG Knives Brochure and Fact File

D. Other Sources

Navy League, "Sea Power, 2000, 2001 Almanacs," Navy League of the United States

Internet Sites for: U.S. Navy Main, SEALs, SEAL Challenge, BUD/S, Warning Order, Navy Recruiting, Len Swiatly

Vietnam BUD/S Class 224, NETPDTC Film Short/NSW – San Diego Electronic Media Center

UDT - SEAL Museum, "Fire in the Hole," various issues